TASTEFUL SCHOOL TIFFIN

DELICIOUS AND NUTRITIOUS RECIPE BOOK

DR GAJANAN SHIRKE

Made with ♥ on the Notion Press Platform
www.notionpress.com

I dedicate this book to mothers of school going childrens and school teachers.

Contents

Preface

Eating right in school made fun and easy for kids now. Do you constantly worry about your child's nutrition and growth, the effects of junk-food overdose and a gadget-centric lifestyle, and the true value of expensive super foods. The book tackles the universal challenge of getting children - vegetarian or not - to enjoy and eat up their veg. Packed with simple, fresh recipes that are nutritious and use vegetables in interesting and inspiring ways, the book is set to lure even the most reticent of eaters. This book is perfect for parents, educators, trying to explain school tiffin to kids.

Acknowledgements

I would like to express a special word of gratitude to my wife Rajeshree and my two daughters Rupeshi & Kavya, my teammates and superior leaders whose encouragement empowered me to write.

ACKNOWLEDGEMENTS

Index

About Author

Dr Gajanan Shirke, a hotel consultant, has an extensive experience over many years in the hospitality industry. His thirst for learning and aspiration to become a multi-faceted expert in the hotel industry helped him to rise from employment to becoming an independent professional in the hospitality sector. Since his last assignment as a General Manager at Kamat Hotels, he has become a renowned hotel
consultant with a proven track record of developing, training and growing some of the best-known hotels, restaurants and fast-food joints in the Indian market. He was appointed as an expert consultant for The Eighth meeting of the Board of Studies for Hotel Management & Catering Technology. He is a visiting faculty at various Hotel Management Colleges and has trained over a thousand hospitality
professionals. He has completed numerous pre and post opening hotel consultancies in India and overseas.

In order to spread his extensive knowledge to aspiring hotel professionals, Gajanan has penned a large number of books spanning different segments of the hospitality industry. Starting from his first book 'Bar Management and Operations' published in 2010, he has written 53 books including Hospitality
Management, Food and Beverage Management, Hotel Engineering Management, Front Office
Management, Hotel Housekeeping Management, Hotel Sales and Marketing, Hospitality Industry Accounting & Fundamentals, Customer Interaction Excellence in Hospitality, History of Indian Cuisine, History of Indian Cuisine Volumes 1 & 2, Hotel Owner's Manual, Hotel Security & Prevention, Training Manager's Manual, Exceptional Service In Hospitality Six Sigma Way and The Cookery Trilogy that consists of Advance Cookery Theory , Foundation of Cookery and The Basic Cookery
Book

CHAPTER ONE

Lunch Time Challenges

Reality is when deliciously prepared lunch come home looking very much like it did when you packed it. Mostly kid's excuse you packed me way too much food and I have to eat quickly. Every school is different, but some children may only get 15-20 minutes to eat their lunch. Most children are not only eating lunch, but also spending that time socializing with friends. For some children this socialization can be an important part of their day. Other factors that can affect a child's intake at lunch time can include:

- A child's desire to not eat foods that are too messy or he doesn't like it.
- I Wasn't Hungry
- I didn't have enough time
- Few preparation that can make eating certain foods difficult
- Being overwhelmed by having too much food packed in the lunch box

Things have not changed much today. Children still wish to not take lunch boxes to schools and rather eat from outside. Moreover, children spend most of their time away from home in schools, classes for different activities which gives them more opportunity to keep hogging on these types of foods.

The following are some Tips that can help parents manage many of these issues:

Avoid over packing. If you pack a lot of food and your child eats it without a problem, then this is not a concern. However, because of a limited amount of time to eat, many children can be overwhelmed by too much food in their lunch boxes. This does not mean that you will need to pack a less nutritious lunch. I recommend packing smaller portions from at least four food groups.

Do not pack multiple containers. Many children will open one container of food at a time and eat it. It may take small children more time to open each container; therefore, if they do not open it (or can't open it), they don't eat it.

Pack the foods that will give them the most nutrition. If you want your child to eat fruits, vegetables, and a protein, then only pack those items. Most children are hungry for lunch. As long as they have been involved in choosing the foods they like in their lunch they will eat them. An example lunch would include a fruit, vegetable, and cottage cheese, cheese, roll-up on whole wheat roti with water to drink. A treat is okay to include in lunch occasionally, but I would recommend only packing small amounts. Packing a small amount will not give a child enough to fill up on it.

CHAPTER TWO

Nutrition Guideline

Eating becomes a social activity in this stage of life. Your kids may spend more time in school than they do at home, eat meals at friends' houses, and adopt eating habits from their peers. It can be difficult to ensure they are getting adequate nutrition when you are not around to monitor their choices, so try to maintain regular family mealtimes.

As children develop, they require the same healthy foods adults eat, along with more vitamins and minerals to support growing bodies. This means whole grains (whole wheat, oats, barley, rice, millet, quinoa); a wide variety of fresh fruits and vegetables; calcium for growing bones (milk, yogurt, or substitutes if lactose intolerant); and healthy proteins (fish, eggs, poultry, lean meat, nuts, and seeds). For kids aged 5-16, the key word is variety. Creative serving ideas will go a long way towards maintaining healthy eating habits.

Every school-going child needs wide variety of fresh foods from five food groups. These groups provide all the nutrients for growth of the body, and energy to function including physical activity.

1. Fruits
2. Vegetables
3. Cereals (grain foods)
4. Dairy
5. Protein

Fruits and Vegetables

- Fruits and vegetables protect us against many diseases, such as heart disease, stroke, and some cancers later in life. Vitamins, water, antioxidants, and fibers are provided by them.
- Fruits and/or vegetables should be included in every meal. Try eating fruits and vegetables of different colors, textures, and tastes.
- Locally grown seasonal fruits and vegetables should be preferred. Whole fruit is better (but after proper cleaning) as its skin has many nutrients and fiber.

- Study shows that people who grow vegetables, eat more of greens. Some children are fussy about eating vegetables and fruits initially but they gradually learn if they see others in family doing so.

Grain Foods

- Chapati, paratha, pohe, breakfast cereals, rice, corn, oats, and millets are all grain foods. Growth and learning, both need energy, which is provided by these foods.
- Chapati and wholegrain breads release energy slowly, and will give the child longer lasting energy and keep him feeling fuller for longer time.

Reduced-fat Dairy Foods

- Milk, cheese, and curd/yoghurt are good sources of protein and calcium, which helps in building strong bones and teeth. Some children do not like taking milk, offer them different preparations of dairy, e.g., drinks of lassi, buttermilk, and cheese or curd/ yoghurt.
- Children who are overweight should preferably have reduced-fat dairy products.

Protein

- Proteins are building material, and are important for your child's growth and muscle development.
- Beans, lentils, chickpeas, tofu, and nuts are proteinrich foods. They also provide vitamins and minerals such as iron, zinc, vitamin B12, and omega-3 fatty acids. Red meat and oily fish are particularly important for child's brain development and learning, and are rich source of iron and omega-3 fatty acids.

  - Vegetarian diet may be deficient in some necessary elements of diet and you have to be vigilant to compensate them by other food items or supplements.
  - If you do not eat meat, chicken, and fish but still eat dairy foods and eggs, it is not difficult to manage.
  - Protein is needed to build and maintain muscles, organs, and immune system. We get protein in diet from eggs and dairy products and also from plant sources, such as lentils, beans, peas, seeds, nuts, whole grains, and some vegetables. Soya products have higher amount of protein.
  - Vitamin B12 is needed for healthy nerves and for blood cells formation. This is found in fortified cereals (wherever available), tofu or tempeh, and in nutritional yeast. Sometimes supplement of vitamin B12 may be needed.
  - Deficiency of zinc can slow a child's growth and impair their immune system. Vegetarian sources of zinc are chickpeas, corn, soybeans, kidney beans, spinach, apricots, prunes, blackberries, raspberries, raisins, kiwi,

bananas, strawberries, wheat-germ, pumpkin seeds, sesame, nuts, and dark chocolate.

- Iron: If iron is deficient, then red blood cells will carry less oxygen throughout body. Give spinach and other green vegetables, kidney beans, lentils and iron-fortified breakfast cereals that provide iron.
- Calcium makes the bones and teeth strong. Vegetarians need foods with extra calcium, such as cereals, orange juice, and soymilk. Since bones grow quickly during childhood and adolescence, if calcium is deficient, a supplement may be needed

Healthy fat: Healthy fats are also important to a child's development. These include monounsaturated fats from plant oils like canola oil, peanut oil, and olive oil, as well as avocados, nuts (like almonds, hazelnuts, and pecans), and seeds (such as pumpkin, sesame; and polyunsaturated fats, including Omega-3 and Omega-6 fatty acids, found in fatty fish, such as salmon, herring, mackerel, anchovies, and sardines, or in unheated sunflower, corn, soybean, and flaxseed oils, and walnuts.

Water: 6-8 glasses each day.

Kids are drinking more soda and sugary beverages (including sugar loaded juices) than ever before — drinks that contribute to obesity risk, dental health problems and poor nutrition. The best bet continues to be water. If your children regularly drink soft drinks, they have a greater risk for a number of health problems, including weaker bones. Many kids consume far too much of these unhealthy drinks when they should be drinking water as their primary beverage. As well as this, when young people consume soft drinks they tend to drink less milk and this means that they may not get enough calcium. This is an important issue during childhood and adolescence, which is a key time for bone growth and development. Now is the time to reset your child's drink habits and make water central.

CHAPTER THREE

Parathas

Leftover or Vegetable Curry Parathas

It's so simple yet delicious and quick to prepare. Mostly children's do not eat vegetables you can prepare vegetable curry and mix it with whole wheat aata.

It's quite filling and goes well with simply thick curd, ketchup and pickle

1. Take Atta, dal or vegetable curry, seasonings if required and ghee in a mixing bowl. Mix well.

You can add onion, coriander and some green chilies finely chopped at this stage for more flavor

2. If you need water add little to make a dough. If it is sticky sprinkle more flour and make a non sticky soft dough. Rest 10 minutes and divide into equal sized balls. Reset 10 more minutes

3. To make paratha, take a ball, flatten evenly by giving it a press against counter top. Dust it generously with flour.

4. Heat pan/ tawa side by side and cook both sides with generous drizzle of oil or ghee until golden spots appear. Press gently while cooking to ensure even browning

SOYA KEEMA PARATHA

Soya keema stuffing with spices, masala flavor to blend well with it to make it tasty and well balanced in taste

METHOD

1. Prepare dough and let it rest while we prepare the soya keema. Boil enough water and soak the soya chura for 10 minutes. Drain,wash it and squeeze the water. Repeat the process once again but with salt this time.
2. Heat a pan with oil and season with fennel, add onion and fry for 2 minutes. Add ginger garlic paste and fry till raw smell goes off. Add chopped tomatoes and salt. Fry till soft
3. Add all the powders and fry till the masala turns mushy. Add the squeezed soya churas
4. Add ¼ cup water to blend the masala well with the soya and cook for 8 minutes (or until water evaporates)in low to medium flame to make a dry soya keema
5. Roll a thick roti and spoon generous amount of the keema and roll into parathas carefully. Cook both sides until golden brown in medium flame with oil drizzled over

NOTES

Soaking and squeezing out twice is a very important step to overcome the soya smell. so follow the step.

Pumpkin Paratha

Pumpkins are an easy vegetable to work with – you can easily puree them and add it to anything – porridge, soup, cookies and more. Whisk Affair uses it to make a fiber and Vitamin A-rich paratha recipe that looks bright and yellow too!

Multi Millet Paneer Paratha

Millets have a whole lot of health benefits like better digestion and essential nutrients like protein and calcium. If you've tried a paratha with multiple grains, the natural next step is a multi millet paratha.

Ingredients:

- 1 cup multi millet mix or you can prepare homemade aata
- 1/4 cup grated paneer / cottage cheese (used homemade)
- 1/4 teaspoon carom seeds / ajwain
- 1/4 teaspoon turmeric powder
- 1 teaspoon ghee + for brushing the paratha
- Whole wheat flour for dusting
- Salt to taste
- 1/4 teaspoon crushed black pepper
- 1/4 teaspoon chaat masala (optional)
- 1/4 cup finely chopped fresh coriander leaves.

Method

1. In a large mixing bowl add the multi millet pan cake mix, grated paneer, salt, carom seeds, turmeric powder, black pepper powder, chaat masala, coriander and 1 teaspoon ghee.
2. Mix everything very well using finger tips
3. Divide the dough into 3-5 equal portions.
4. Take each dough ball between the palms, slightly flatten it and using a rolling pin, roll it on a dusted platform into a round shape.
5. Carefully transfer the rolled out paratha to a heated skillet and cook the paratha from both sides until light brown spots appear on the surface
6. Brush the paratha with ghee
7. Serve the multi millet paneer paratha warm with curd, pickle

SPROUTS BROCCOLI or Cauliflower PARATHA

Sprouts broccoli/cauliflower stuffed paratha with moong sprouts and broccoli/Cauliflower cooked with spices to make it suitable for Indian taste buds. The dough also is made spicy to make it extra delicious and tasty.

STEP BY STEP GUIDELINE

1. Take flour, salt, chilli powder, turmeric powder, ghee/ oil and ajwain firstly in a mixing bowl, mix well.
2. After that, add lukewarm water little by little. Make smooth, soft dough. Keep aside for 10 mins. Divide into 5 equal sized balls.
3. Wash and pat dry broccoli. In a mixer, pulse broccoli florets few times.
4. In a pan, heat oil. Splutter cumin in low flame, add finely chopped ginger, asafoetida. Add finely chopped onion. Fry for a minute.
5. Add broccoli and sprouts. Give it a fry. Add chilli powder, turmeric, coriander seeds powder, garam masala powder, required salt.
6. Cook in medium flame for 2 minutes. Broccoli and sprouts should get soft.
7. Spread the dough ball into a thick palm size disc. Take same, dough ball size, of the stuffing.
8. Cover from all sides like we cover modak. Pinch off excess dough if any on the top. Flatten and dust well.
9. Spread evenly to parathas. Dust while rolling to avoid sticking.
10. Heat tawa and cook parathas both sides. Add ghee/ oil on top while cooking.
11. Serve hot with raita and pickle.

Mixed Nuts Paratha

Ingredients:
Wheat flour – 2 cups

- Jaggery – 1/4 cup
- Desiccated coconut – 1/4 Cup
- Mixed nuts powder – 2 tbsp
- Cardamom powder – a pinch
- Ghee – 1 tbsp

Method

1. Knead the wheat flour using ghee and water.
2. Form a dough and keep it aside for 10 minutes
3. For stuffing- Add Mixed nuts powder, jaggery, desiccated coconut and cardamom and Mix well

4. Pinch a small portion of dough and make it into cups
5. Add stuffing in the dough and gather the sides towards the center and pinch the edges together to seal it
6. Roll out the stuffed dough-ball into a thick parathas
7. Cook the paratha over a heated skillet till both sides are cooked and brown
8. Drizzle some ghee over the paratha as you cook it.

Mixed Nuts Paratha is very simple to make and it can also be served as an energy rich after school snack for kids. Kids would definitely love the nutty flavor and sweet taste of these homemade parathas.

OATS PARATHA

Oats Paratha is a healthy and nutritious flat bread made with the goodness of oats, whole wheat flour, veggies and spices. Tastes great with a side of pickle and yogurt.

Ingredient:

oats– I used instant oats, old fashioned oats can also be used.

veggies – I used cabbage and carrot. You can also add bell pepper and potato.

STEP BY STEP INSTRUCTIONS:

1 – Add the oats to a blender and make fine powder.

2- Transfer the powdered oats in to a large bowl and add the whole wheat flour, veggies, spices, salt and oil.

3 & 4 – Mix it well and add just enough water to make a dough.

5- Make a dough which is soft and smooth but not sticky. Cover it and let the dough rest for 15 minutes.

6- After the dough is rested, divide it in to 5 to 6 equal sized balls.

Tastes great with a side of pickle and yogurt.

Rajgira Paratha

Makes 2 *parathas*

Ingredients

- 1/2 cup *rajgira* flour (*cholai/ramdaana*)
- 1/8 cup boiled, peeled and mashed potatoes
- 1 tbsp finely chopped coriander
- 1/4 tsp freshly ground black pepper (*kalimirch*) powder
- Salt to taste
- *Rajgira* flour (*cholai/ramdaana*) for rolling
- Oil for cooking

Method

- Combine the *rajgira* flour, potatoes, salt and pepper in a bowl and knead them into a semi-soft dough using a little water.

- Divide the dough into 4 equal portions and roll out each portion into a *roti*, using a little *rajgira* flour for rolling.
- Heat a non-stick griddle (*tava*) and cook the *paratha*, using a little oil, till it turns golden brown on both sides.
- Serve immediately with green *chutney* and yoghurt.

Raw Papaya *Paratha*

Makes 4 *parathas*

Ingredients

- 200 g whole wheat flour (*gehun ka atta*)
- 1 small raw papaya, peeled and grated
- 2 – 3 green chillies, finely chopped
- 1 tsp cumin seeds (*jeera*)
- 2 tsp coriander leaves
- 1 tsp chilli powder
- 1 tsp dried mango powder (*amchur*)
- 1 tsp *garam masala*
- Salt to taste
- Oil for cooking

Method

- Add a little water to the flour and knead it into a soft dough. Cover it and keep it aside for 30 minutes.
- In another bowl, squeeze out the excess water from the papaya, add the remaining ingredients to it and mix well.
- Divide the dough into 4 equal portions.
- Divide the stuffing into 4 equal portions.
- Roll out a portion of the dough into a circle, 4 inches in diameter.
- Place one portion of the stuffing in the centre and bring the edges together in the middle to seal it tightly. Roll it out again.
- Heat a griddle (*tava*) and cook each *paratha*, using a little oil.

Other Stuff Paratha Options

1. Nutrella or Peanut Butter Paratha : Is your kid bored of the regular parathas you serve? Make this simple and delicious paratha for kids that your children will simply love. If you're craving chocolate, this is the great recipe for Nutella Lovers!
2. Cabbage Paratha: A healthy, easy paratha made by adding grated cabbage and spices directly into the dough.
3. Cheese and Corn Paratha : mashed corn and cheese parathas with pizza seasoning
4. Mix Vegetable Stuffed Paratha: Stuffed with seasonal tossed kheema vegetable you can add paneer
5. Mushroom and Hara Pyaaz Ka Paratha : stuffed with mushroom and hara pyaaz

6. Rajma aur Beetroot Ka stuffed Paratha : is a healthy and delicious flat bread that is with Rajma and Beetroot chatpata stuffing.
7. Paneer Chilli Stuffed Paratha: Can mix Panner chilli in dough and prepare parathas
8. Aachari Paratha (Mango Pickle Masala Paratha) is a spicy and delicious flatbread. It is prepared using wheat flour and pickle masala.

CHAPTER FOUR

Dressings and Sauce

Olive oil

Sometimes all a salad needs is a drizzle of some really good olive oil. A little fat is never a bad thing. In fact, research actually found that full-fat salad dressings may help the body better absorb certain nutrients (specifically carotenoids).Trusted Source

Plus, it's high in omega-3s, including oleic acid. These play an essential role in keeping brain cells healthy. It's also high in phytochemicals, antioxidants.

Fruit n' nut delight: There's nothing better than making a dressing packed with whole-foods! It's like adding more nutrition via your sauce. Get all the benefits of whole-fruit and nuts by mixing them into a dressing. The addition of nuts also creates creaminess while adding some heart-healthy fats and fiber.

Try blending:

- 1/3 cup chopped nuts
- 1/2 cup chopped fresh fruit
- 1/4 cup unsweetened soy or almond milk
- 1 tablespoon lemon or lime juice

Roasted tomato vinaigrette

Any dressing that has another serving of whole vegetables gets an A+ in our books. The addition of whole roasted tomatoes to this dressing recipe not only adds tons of great nutrients but also achieves an awesome hearty texture. Plus, tomatoes are a great source of lycopene, a carotenoid (antioxidant) that's been associated with everything from a reduced risk of prostate cancer,Trusted Source all the way to preventing cardiovascular disease.Trusted Source

The basics

- 12 ounces plum tomatoes
- 1 tablespoon garlic

- 1 teaspoon Italian seasoning
- 2 tablespoons vinegar
- It's a perfect topper for a green salad or roasted veggies or meat.

Classic lemon vinaigrette

Emeril Lagasse has it right with this one. His salt-free recipe recreates that classic French vinaigrette flavor without maxing out your daily sodium intake.

Just mush together the following ingredients in a blender:

- 2 tablespoons fresh herbs, including parsley, tarragon, chives, and oregano
- 1 tablespoon shallots, minced
- 1 teaspoon garlic, minced
- lemon and lime zest
- 1 tablespoons Dijon mustard
- 2 tablespoons lemon juice
- 1/4 cup oil

Sweet honey dressing

Sometimes fruit needs a little dressing too, right?

Try blending up the following ingredients:

- 1 cup plain Greek yogurt
- 2 tablespoons honey (or agave)
- 1 tablespoon grated orange zest
- the juice from 1/2 a lemon
- You get the sweetness and the citrus kick, as well as the richness of the yogurt.

Green goddess

This classic avocado dressing is perfect for summer (well, it's perfect anytime, but the mint and cilantro give it a summery tang).

Blend:

- the meat of 1 avocado
- 1 1/2 cup fat-free buttermilk
- 1/4 cup fresh herbs (tarragon, mint, parsley, and cilantro work well)

- 2 tablespoons rice vinegar until smooth.

Maple mustard dressing: Tangy. Sweet. Who doesn't love the combo of maple and mustard? This dressing is the perfect combo and goes well with any hearty salad —especially mixed greens with goat cheese, pecans, and beets.

Plus it's easy to throw together. Just blend up:

- 2 tablespoons coarse-grain mustard
- 1/4 cup maple syrup
- 1/2 cup walnut or canola oil
- 1/4 cup apple cider vinegar
- 2 tablespoons soy sauce
- sprinkling of salt and pepper

Classic honey mustard

We'll dip anything in honey mustard dressing.

Ingredients:

- 2 tablespoons apple cider vinegar
- 2 tablespoons Dijon mustard
- 1 tablespoon honey
- 1/2 cup olive oil
- Simply citrus

Fresh citrus juice is a perfect accompaniment to greens. It just makes them pop. A mix of juices (orange, grapefruit, lemon, and lime) is what makes this dressing even more special that your average.

Combine 3 tablespoons of each citrus juice with 1 1/2 cups olive oil, and add salt and pepper to taste. Shake or whisk the whole shebang until it's well combined.

And that's it. If your salad's full of nuts, you'll absolutely love drizzling this zingy concoction over the top.

Yogurt herb Dijon spread

Non-fat Greek yogurt is a great way to get a creamy dressing without the extra fat (and it adds an extra dose of protein to boot).

Mix the following:

- 1/2 cup plain Greek yogurt
- 2 tablespoons Dijon mustard

- 1/4 cup chopped fresh herbs

Hummus

Hummus is another great alternative to mayo. It's just as creamy, even more flavorful, and offers a little extra protein and fiber. Just be careful not to overdo it! More than 1 tablespoon or 2 and this spread can get a little calorie-heavy.

Ingredients

For Pressure Cooking Chickpeas

- ½ cup heaped dried white chickpeas, 120 grams soaked in enough water for 8 to 9 hours or overnight
- 1.5 cups water
- ½ teaspoon salt
- 1 pinch baking soda

Other Ingredients

- 3 tablespoons white sesame seeds or 2 tablespoons tahini
- 4 tablespoons extra virgin olive oil
- 1 teaspoon chopped garlic or 4 to 5 small to medium garlic cloves, chopped
- 1 to 2 tablespoons lemon juice
- 1 teaspoon cumin powder
- salt as required

For Garnishing

- extra virgin olive oil, as required
- red chili powder or paprika or cayenne pepper – as required
- black pepper powder, as required – optional
- a few sprigs of parsley or coriander leaves (cilantro leaves)

Instructions

Cooking Dried Chickpeas

- Rinse ½ heaped cup dried chickpeas (120 grams) in water first and then soak in enough water overnight or for 8 to 9 hours.

- Next day, rinse the chickpeas in water first a couple of times. Drain all the water and add the chickpeas in a 2 litre stovetop pressure cooker.
- Add ½ teaspoon salt, 1 pinch of baking soda and 1.5 cups water.
- Pressure cook on medium heat for 11 to 12 minutes.
- When the pressure settles down on its own in the cooker, remove the lid and check the chickpeas.
- Mash them with a spoon or with your fingers. You should be able to mash them completely. They should have no rawness in them. You can even taste them and there should be no bite in them. They should melt in the mouth.
- If the chickpeas are not cooked properly, then add some more water and pressure cook for some more time. Drain all the water. Cover and keep aside.

Roasting Sesame Seeds

- Heat a small pan. Keep heat to a low. Add 3 tablespoons white sesame seeds.
- On a low heat stirring often roast sesame seeds.
- Roast till they become crisp and start crackling. No need to brown them. Let them cool down.

Making Hummus

- In a food processor, mixer-grinder-blender or food chopper take the roasted sesame seeds.
- Powder it to fine or semi-fine texture.
- Add 1 teaspoon chopped garlic, 1 to 2 tablespoons lemon juice, 4 tablespoons extra virgin olive oil, 1 teaspoon cumin powder and salt as per taste.
- 1 tablespoons lemon juice works fine for us. To increase the tang more, you can add overall 2 tablespoons lemon juice. So add as per your taste.
- Add salt as per taste. Do note that the chickpeas will also have some salty taste in them as salt was used when cooking chickpeas. So add less salt first. Later you can add more salt if required.
- Grind or blend to a fine or semi-fine consistency.
- Next add the cooked chickpeas.
- Grind or blend till smooth and light. If you are unable to grind, then add 2 to 3 tablespoons water.

Serving Hummus

- Hummus is ready now and all you need is to scrape the jar and place it in a serving bowl or bowls. Make a round pattern with a spoon on the hummus.

- Drizzle a bit of extra virgin olive oil. Sprinkle paprika or red chilli powder or black pepper powder or any of your favorite spice powder. You can also sprinkle zatar. Garnish with a few chopped coriander leaves or parsley leaves.
- Serve it with warm pita bread or with steamed or roasted veggies. The extra hummus can be stored in an air-tight container in the refrigerator.

In place of olive oil, you can use neutral tasting oil like sunflower oil.

Instead of dried chickpeas, you can use 2 cups cooked chickpeas or canned chickpeas in the recipe.

Vanilla almond butter

When you want a high fiber, protein-packed snack, try using this vanilla almond butter on the classic PB&J instead of the standard peanut butter.

This recipe uses only five ingredients:

- 2 cups raw almonds
- 2 cups roasted, unsalted cashews
- 2 tablespoons coconut oil
- 1 teaspoon vanilla extract
- 1 or 2 tablespoons honey
- Take all that with a pinch of salt (literally) and blend it.

Pesto

Basic pesto can turn any panini or grilled cheese into something a bit fancier

Just blend up:

- 2 bunches fresh basil
- 2 sun-dried tomatoes
- 5 cloves garlic
- 3/4 cup of EVOO (extra virgin olive oil)
- Blend them until smooth and... hey presto! Pesto.
- If you're not so crazy about the pungent garlic flavor, roast it first.

You can Add Roasted: Walnuts / Cashunuts / Pine Nuts / SUnflower Seeds / Melon Seeds

Green mayo

Don't run away just yet, though.

We're not so crazy about mayonnaise by itself, but throwing in a dose of greens makes anything a bit healthier (for those who really can't get enough mayo) (there's definitely such a thing as enough mayo, by the way).

- 75 grams spinach
- 40 grams watercress
- 40 grams parsley
- 2 tablespoons chopped tarragon
- 1 tablespoon chives
- Throw in a splash of lemon juice and a dash of salt and pepper, and this one comes with the Greatist seal of approval.

Mojito mbharinade

A marinade with rum in it.
Try a mix of:

- 2 shallots
- 1/4 cup mint
- 1/4 cup rum
- 1/2 cup lime juice
- Throw in some lime zest, salt, and canola oil for a festive flavoring.

Classic Indian

Want tasty tandoori chicken from any oven or grill? It's easy. (And no, you don't need to buy a Tandoor oven.)
Marinate Paneer:

- 1/2 cup plain Greek yogurt or hung curd
- 2 tablespoons olive oil
- 1 teaspoon ground cumin
- 1 teaspoon ground turmeric
- 1/2 teaspoon ground coriander

Easy teriyaki

Simply mix:

- 1/3 cup water
- 1/3 cup brown sugar
- 1/3 cup soy sauce
- 1 crushed clove garlic

- 1/2 teaspoon cinnamon

Dijon sun-dried tomato

This is a Greatest family favorite.
Combine:

- 1 teaspoon thyme
- 1 teaspoon rosemary
- 1/4 cup olive oil
- 2 sun-dried tomatoes in oil
- 1 tablespoon Dijon mustard
- Spread the whole business on top of salmon or chicken, and bake until cooked through. Voila! Deliciousness.

Turkish delight

Combine:

- 1 cup plain Greek yogurt
- the juice and zest of 1 lemon
- 1 cup chopped fresh mint
- 2 cloves garlic, minced
- a sprinkle of salt
- 1/2 teaspoon cinnamon
- 1/2 teaspoon cayenne
- 1/4 teaspoon ground allspice
- Mix and marinate the meat for anywhere between 1 and 4 hours. Grill it for the best results.

Rosemary balsamic

Mix together:

- 2 tablespoons olive oil
- 2 tablespoons balsamic vinegar
- 6 garlic cloves
- 6 fresh rosemary sprigs
- a hearty grind of pepper
- Marinate for up to 24 hours (that's a long soak but it's worth it) and grill or bake for a soft, fragrant, tender cook.

Classic chipotle

combine:

- 1 chipotle in adobo
- 3 cloves garlic, minced
- the juice of 1 lime
- 1 teaspoon vinegar (of your choice)
- Marinate the mixture overnight for maximum impact.

Honey lime marinade

Combine:

- 1/2 cup honey
- 1/3 cup reduced sodium soy sauce
- the juice of 2 limes

CHAPTER FIVE

Roti or Paratha Rolls & Wraps

Delicious wraps or rolls stuffed with a spiced mix veg or seasonal vegetables and nuts stuffing. These roll make for a good brunch, lunch or tiffin box snack or a portable meal on the go!

Tawa Roti Quesadilla

Tawa Roti quesadilla is a nice variation from the regular Tawa Roti and sabji. The stuffing is already inside the Tawa Roti ,with the melted cheese. Its a mess free lunch box recipe. Cut the quesadilla into triangles, and serve with some salsa.

Ingredients:

- Slice onion- 3 tbsp
- Sliced bell pepper- ½ cup
- Cooked black beans- ½ cup
- Cumin power- ¼ tsp
- Coriander power- ½ tsp
- Red chilly power- ½ tsp or to taste
- Lemon juice to taste
- Salt to taste
- Freshly chopped coriander leaves
- Grated cheese- few teaspoons
- Four chapati
- Oil- 3 tsps

Procedure to make Tawa Roti quesadilla:
Making the filling for the Tawa Roti quesadilla-

1. Heat a pan and add the oil. When the oil gets hot,add the sliced onion and cook till lightly soft.

2. Add the bell pepper and some salt. Cook till the peppers and onion turn soft.
3. Add the black beans, cumin powder, coriander powder, red chilly powder and salt.
4. Mix well and with the back of the spoon mash the black beans.
5. Cook for five minutes.
6. Finally add the lemon juice, coriander leaves and salt and switch of the flame.
7. **making the Tawa Roti quesadilla-**

1. Heat a pan in low flame and place one Tawa Roti on it.
2. Add some grated cheese and add little filling and spread it evenly.
3. Top it with more cheese and close it with the other Tawa Roti .
4. Increase the heat to medium and cook the queadilla by pressing the the Tawa Roti with a spatula.
5. Cook on both sides till the cheese melts.
6. Cool the Tawa Roti and cut them to four slices and pack for lunch box.

Rainbow Wrap

Method:

- In this wrap, the hummus is spread onto the tortilla or roti.
- The fillings inside will be shredded purple cabbage, carrot, lettuce, and sliced tomatoes and bell peppers.
- Drizzle vinaigrette onto the fillings and wrap it neatly and serve.

Mediterranean Wrap

Method:

- Chickpeas are soaked the previous night, and they are drained and blended into a smooth paste.
- Then hummus is spread onto the tortilla or Roti . On top of this, another layer of the chickpeas paste is applied.
- Spread baby lettuce on the tortilla or roti , and then sliced cucumber, plum tomato, and avocado are placed on it.
- Olives are sprinkled, and one tablespoon of vinaigrette is sufficiently sprinkled.
- Then the wrap is rolled and served with a sauce of your choice.

Banana Wrap

Method:

- This is made by first spreading a seed butter or any favourite nut butter on the tortilla or roti.
- Then peel and slice the bananas. Please place them in the centre of the tortilla or roti.

- You can add Nutrela / chocolate syrup / peanut butter
- Wrap it and serve it immediately.
- This can be refrigerated also and then consumed.

RED KIDNEY BEANS AND CHEESE BURRITO

Bean and Cheese Burrito inspired Rajma chawal (red kidney beans curry and rice) and cheese rolled in homemade chapati (whole wheat flatbread). Lightly toast it till cheese melts. Packed with chocolate-flavored coconut rolls from sprouts and cucumber and cherry tomatoes.

Corn and Spinach Wrap

Ingredients

- One cup boiled and crushed corn
- Half cup spinach cooked with garlic and seasonings
- Half cup mashed potato
- 2 table spoon chopped coriander
- 1 tea spoon green chilli chop
- Salt to taste
- 2 spoon oil
- Leftover chapatti
- 1 cup lettuce
- 4 table spoon mayonnaise (you can use flavoured or plain)

Method

- Combine all ingredients in one ball mix well
- Take a chapatti
- Spread mayonnaise
- Add mixture and roll it in a silver foil or butter pepper

Making Roll Stuffing

1. Heat 2 tablespoons oil in a pan or kadai. You can use any neutral-flavored oil.
Then add ¼ teaspoon ajwain (carom seeds) and ¼ teaspoon cumin seeds. Let them splutter.
2. Then add ⅓ cup finely chopped onions
3. Saute stirring often till the onions turn translucent.
4. Add 1 teaspoon ginger-garlic paste.

5. Stir and saute for a few seconds or till the raw aroma of both ginger and garlic goes away.
6. Add ½ cup chopped tomatoes.
7. Mix well and saute the tomatoes on a low to medium heat for 3 minutes or till they soften.
8. Then add the following ground spices and mix very well.

- ¼ teaspoon turmeric powder
- ½ teaspoon Kashmiri red chilli powder (If using regular red chili powder, then add ¼ teaspoon of it.)
- ½ teaspoon coriander powder
- ½ teaspoon garam masala powder.

You can vary the amount of spices as per your taste buds.

9. Then add ⅓ cup chopped capsicum cubes.
10. Sauté for two or three minutes.
11. Next add all the steamed veggies. If there is any water in the pan of the steamed veggies, then add this water too. Also add salt as per taste.
12. Mix very well.
13. on a low to medium heat sauté for 4 to 5 minutes. Do make sure that the veg stuffing is dry.
14. Next add ¼ cup of chopped coriander leaves. Mix very well.
15. Lastly add ¼ cup grated or crumbled Paneer. Paneer is optional and you can skip it. Check the taste and add more salt or chili powder if required. Mix very well and keep the veg stuffing aside.

Stuffing : you can add vegetables / Cottage cheese / Mushrooms / Beans / Soya Chunks / Tofu /Paneer Tikka / Mushroom Tikka / Grilled Pineapple and Vegetables

Dressings: You can prepare homemade chutnies or can prepare mayo base sauce – can add Chopped pickled vegetables , chopped cucumber, Spice mixes based on kids likes, fresh seasonings like Coriander , Basil , Thyme , Burned Garlic , readymade sauces , mustered , honey , roasted nuts ,bottled salad dressings like ranch, honey mustard, or Italian , mustard , mayonnaise , guacamole , hummus , cream cheese , basil pesto , nut or seed butter

Vegetables: Cucumber Julian's seedless, Tomato Julian's seedless, lightly sautéed onion, Lettuce

Fruits: banana slices/ berries /apple slices / pear slices / all fruit jam / raisins / dried cranberries / peaches or nectarines

Seeds & Nuts (Roasted/Plain): Sunflower Seeds / Pumpkin Seeds / Melon Seeds / Roasted Almond / Roasted Pista / Roasted Peanuts / Roasted Cashew nuts / Pine nuts

Proteins: Peanut or almond butter, re-fried beans, cooked ground turkey , ricotta cheese, black or kidney beans

CHAPTER SIX

Sandwiches

Grilled Peanut Butter and Jelly Sandwich

Ingredients

- 1 tablespoon unsalted butter, softened
- 2 slices sandwich bread
- 2 tablespoons peanut butter or other nut butter
- 1 tablespoon jam, jelly or fruit preserves

Directions

1. Heat a skillet over medium heat. Spread the butter on one side of each slice of bread. Spread the peanut butter on the unbuttered side of one slice of bread. Repeat with the jelly on the remaining slice of bread. Assemble the sandwich with the peanut butter and jelly inside.

2. Place the sandwich in the skillet and cook until golden brown, about 5 minutes. Flip the sandwich and cook until the second side is golden brown, about 5 minutes more. Remove from the skillet, cool slightly and cut into triangles before serving.

Chickpea Salad Sandwich

Ingredients

Ingredient Checklist

- 2 (15.5 ounce) cans no-salt-added chickpeas, rinsed
- 6 tablespoons extra-virgin olive oil
- 3 tablespoons lemon juice
- 2 teaspoons Dijon mustard
- ½ teaspoon garlic powder
- ½ cup finely chopped celery
- ¼ cup finely chopped fresh dill

- ⅛ teaspoon salt
- ⅛ teaspoon ground pepper
- 4 tablespoons vegan mayonnaise
- 8 slices whole-grain bread, toasted
- 4 green lettuce leaves
- 4 thin slices red onion
- 4 tomato slices

Directions

- Combine chickpeas, oil, lemon juice, mustard and garlic powder in a large bowl. Using a fork or potato masher, crush the chickpeas until most are mashed but some are still whole. Stir in celery, dill, salt and pepper.
- Spread 1 tablespoon mayonnaise on 1 side of each of 4 slices of bread. Top evenly with lettuce, onion, tomato and chickpea mixture. Top with the remaining 4 slices of bread.

Mushrooms, Corn And Cheese Sandwich

Cheese, being a dairy product, is usually high in protein, but make sure you pick the right kind of cheese. Mozzarella cheese is said to be a healthier option when compared to cheddar or parmesan. One can find mozzarella quite easily nowadays. Put together some boiled mushrooms, boiled corns and shredded mozzarella cheese on top of your bread slice and grill.

Soya Sandwich

Ingredients

- Carrots - 1 no
- Boiled soya granules - 100gms
- Coriander leaves
- Brown Bread
- Chopped onions - 1 no
- Chopped tomatoes - 1 no
- Green chilli
- Chopped capsicum - 1 no

Method:

- Take olive oil in a pan.
- Then, add boiled soya granules and all the veggies.

- And spices like salt, black pepper, oregano basil, and chili flakes.
- Then, cook properly like sautee all the veggies.
- And, then put this mixture inside the two bread slices and grill it.

Health Benefits of high protein soya sandwich recipe

- Soybean is rich in folic acid and vitamin B complex that is essential for pregnant women
- Also, soybeans can help in reducing the occurrence of insomnia along with other sleeping disorders
- Brown bread is a good source of vitamin E, vitamin B, and vitamin K.
- Also, brown bread acts as a natural laxative and helps in better bowel movements.
- Spring onions have carotenoids which help to keep the vision healthy and intact.
- Also, it is rich in vitamin A which prevents loss of eyesight.
- Carrots are about 10% carbs, consisting of starch, and simple sugars.

Hummus Veggie Sandwich

Hummus is made with chickpeas, olive oil, garlic, tahini, lemon juice and salt.

INGREDIENTS

- 4 pieces hearty whole grain sandwich bread
- Hummus
- Fresh spinach leaves
- 1 large carrot, grated
- 4 large ripe tomato slices
- 1 ripe avocado, sliced
- Thinly sliced red onion
- Alfalfa sprouts
- Salt and pepper to taste

INSTRUCTIONS

1. Prepare all your ingredients. You can toast the bread if you like in a toaster or leave it untoasted.
2. Add a thick layer of hummus to the inside all each piece of bread. On two pieces of bread add a thin layer of fresh spinach leaves. Top with grated carrot, then tomato slices, add some salt and pepper to the tomato slices, then add avocado, then red onion, then alfalfa sprouts.
3. Add the second piece of bread, hummus side down. Slice in half and serve right away.

VEGGIE CHICKPEA SALAD SANDWICH

INGREDIENTS

FOR THE SALAD:

- 15 oz canned chickpeas, drained + rinsed
- 3 stalks green onion
- 2 stalks celery
- 1/4 cup chopped shredded carrots
- 1/4 cup finely chopped red bell pepper
- 1/4 cup finely chopped dill pickle
- 1/4 cup store bought or homemade mayonnaise vegan or regular
- 1-2 tsp dijon mustard
- 1 tsp yellow mustard
- 1/8 tsp dried dill or fresh, to taste
- 1/8 tsp salt
- 1/8 tsp pepper
- 3 TBSP unsalted roasted sunflower seeds
- 2 TBSP fresh chopped basil plus extra to taste

FOR THE SANDWICH:

- multi-grain sandwich bread
- arugula or romaine lettuce
- extra basil as desired
- optional tomatoes and/or red onion

TASTY SANDWICH SPREAD OPTIONS

- spicy mustard
- hummus
- mayo

INSTRUCTIONS

- Drain and rinse your chickpeas and add them to a large bowl. Mash with a potato masher until texture appears flaked, almost like tuna salad. I use both a potato masher and follow up with a fork to make sure every chickpea is deliciously smashed. You could also use a food processor and skip the arm workout!
- Chop your green onion, celery, shredded carrots, pepper, and pickles.
- Add to the bowl with your chickpeas, then add mayo, dijon, yellow mustard, dill, salt, and pepper. Stir well to coat.
- Fold in sunflower seeds and basil (as much or as little as you'd like) and adjust any ingredients to taste.
- Pile high on bread with all your sandwich fixings or enjoy as a wrap, with crackers, on a salad, or simply dive into the bowl spoon-first – anything goes!

Cheesy Sandwich

When your child is not happy with too many ingredients in his sandwich filling, you can try this one. It has lots of cheese and some greens.

You will need:

- 8 slices of bread
- 1 head broccoli, separated into florets
- 1 cup cheddar cheese, grated or thinly sliced
- 2 tablespoons olive oil
- Salt to taste
- Softened, unsalted butter
- ¼ teaspoon crushed black pepper

How to:

1. Preheat the oven to 400°F.
2. In an oven sheet, add olive oil, salt and pepper, and the broccoli florets. Bake them for around ten minutes and set aside.
3. Heat a skillet on the stove. Apply butter to one side of a bread slice and put it in the skillet, with the buttered side down.
4. Spread one layer of cheese. Top it with the broccoli florets and add another layer of cheese on it.
5. Let the cheese melt a little, before covering it with another slice of bread.
6. Cook both sides of the sandwich for five minutes each, until the cheese melts enough to hold the slices together.
7. Cut the sandwich in half and serve with ketchup.

Cucumber Cream Cheese Sandwiches

Cucumber is a natural body coolant. Combine it with cream cheese, and you have a healthy, creamy vegetable sandwich for kids.

You will need:

- 6 slices whole grain bread
- 4 ounces cream cheese
- ½ cucumber seeded and sliced thinly
- Juice and zest of one lemon
- 2 tablespoons fresh dill
- Salted butter
- Black pepper, ground
- Salt to taste

How to:

1. Tap dry the thinly sliced cucumber with a paper towel. Set them aside.
2. Mix the cream cheese, dill, lemon zest and juice, salt and pepper in a bowl.
3. Butter one side of the bread slices and spread the cream cheese mix on top.
4. Top three slices of bread with the cucumber slices, you can add two-three slices.
5. Cover the cucumber with the remaining bread slices and cut off the edges.
6. Cut the bread slices into equal triangles and serve.

Carrot And Peanut Butter Sandwich

Peanut butter is rich in protein. But if you want more than that, you can add a veggie to the sandwich spread.

You will need:

- ¼ cup creamy peanut butter
- ½ cup finely shredded carrot
- 1 tablespoon apricot marmalade
- 2 teaspoons raisins

How to:

1. Mix the peanut butter, raisins, grated carrots, and marmalade in a bowl. Whisk it well to make a creamy spread.
2. Use the sandwich spread on bread, tortilla rolls, or bun for a healthy snack.

Roasted Pumpkin Sandwich

Pumpkin is rich in essential nutrients that your child needs to stay healthy.

You will need:

- 100 grams pumpkin
- ½ avocado
- 1 carrot, small
- 4 slices whole grain bread
- 1 large iceberg lettuce leaf

How to:

1. Preheat the oven to 160°Fahrenheit.
2. Peel the pumpkin and remove the seeds. Put the pumpkin on a baking tray or sheet and cook for ten minutes. Once done, let it cool and slice it thinly.
3. Peel the avocado and remove the seed. Mash it lightly in a bowl, using a fork.
4. Spread the avocado paste on two bread slices. Top it with grated carrot, lettuce leaf, and pumpkin slices.
5. Cover with the remaining two bread slices to complete the sandwich.

Cheese and Peanut Butter Sandwich

You will need:

- 2 slices bread
- 2tbsp peanut butter
- 1 slice cheddar cheese
- 2tsp margarine

How to:

1. Spread the peanut butter on one side of a bread slice.
2. Top it with the cheese slice and cover with the other slice of bread.
3. Apply butter on both sides of the sandwich and cook it in the skillet for three-five minutes or until the cheese melts.
4. Cut into diagonal triangles and serve.

Cinnamon-Raisin Peanut Butter Sandwich

This is a simple peanut butter sandwich, flavored with cinnamon and enriched with raisins.

You will need:

- ½ cup peanut butter
- 2tbsp honey
- 2tbsp raisins
- 8 slices whole grain bread
- 2tsp ground cinnamon

How to:

1. Mix the peanut butter, raisins, and honey in a bowl.
2. Spread the mix on four slices of bread and sprinkle the raisins on top.
3. Place the other bread slices on top to make the sandwich.
4. You can cut it into small cubes or triangles before serving.

Bombay Masala Sandwich

Ingredients:
8 slices of whole-wheat Bread
For the filling:

- 2 medium potato, boiled, peeled and mashed
- ¼ cup green peas
- 1 green chilli, minced
- ½ tsp cumin seeds
- A sprig of curry leaves
- 1 tbsp oil
- ½ tsp red chilli powder
- Salt to taste
- ½ tsp garam masala
- Handful of chopped coriander leaves
- To assemble
- Thin tomato slices
- Thin onion slices

- Chaat masala to sprinkle
- 2 cubes Amul cheese
- 4 tbsp green chutney
- Butter to brush the bread slices

Method:

1. Heat a pan and add oil. Add cumin seeds and curry leaves and let them splutter for a few seconds
2. Add the mashed potato, peas, salt and red chilli powder and mix well. Cover and let it cook for 2-3 minutes.
3. Add garam masala and the chopped coriander leaves and mix again. Take it off heat and let it cool a bit.
4. On one side of each bread slice smear the green chutney. On half of the slices spread the prepared potato mixture in a thin layer. Spread a layer of tomato slices and onion slices. Sprinkle some chaat masala and spread a layer of grated cheese.
5. Cover it with another bread slice with the green chutney side down. Repeat the same with the rest of the slices.
6. On the outer sides of the prepared sandwich, apply butter generously and grill them in a preheated sandwich maker till they are crisp and golden lines form on the outer side.
7. Serve hot with green chutney and tomato ketchup. Enjoy with a cup of masala chai or coffee.

Note: You can also add thin slices of capsicum along with tomato and onion slices.

Peanut Butter and Banana Sandwich

Ingredients

- 2 to 3 ripe bananas
- 8 slices white bread
- 3/4 cup crunchy peanut butter
- 3 tablespoons honey
- 1 1/2 teaspoons plus 1 tablespoon for topping cinnamon
- 1/2 cup butter
- 1/4 cup sugar

Directions

In frying pan melt 3 tablespoons of butter – make sure butter does not burn. In a small bowl mix together peanut butter, honey and cinnamon. Slice bananas into 1/4″ thick slices. Spread the peanut butter mixture on four slices of bread and cover with banana slices. Top with remaining 4 slices of bread. Spread butter on both sides of sandwiches. Grill sandwiches in frying pan until each side is golden brown.

For topping, combine sugar cinnamon in shallow plate. Coat grilled sandwiches with mixture.

FRUIT SANDWICH

INGREDIENTS

- 8 sliced white bread 1 cm (1/2 inch) thick
- 300 ml heavy cream (double cream) chilled
- 1 1/2 tbsp granulated / caster sugar
- 1 tbsp sweetened condensed milk

FRUIT OF YOUR CHOICE (I USED BELOW)

- 1 banana
- 1 kiwi fruit
- 1 orange
- 12 small strawberries

INSTRUCTIONS

1. Prepare the fruit. Banana and kiwi: peel and cut into bite size pieces. Strawberries: remove the calyx. Orange: peel the outside and inside skin. Pat the fruit with a paper towel to remove excess water.
2. Place the sugar and the heavy cream (double cream) in a large bowl and beat with an electric beater until soft peaks.
3. Add the sweetened condensed milk and beat until firm peaks.
4. Spread the cream evenly on one side of each slice of bread.
5. Arrange the fruit over the cream on one side of 4 sliced bread with an awareness of how to look the cut section of the fruit.
6. Put some more whipped cream on the fruit, filling the gap between the fruit.
7. Cover the fillings with the other slice of bread. Then wrap each sandwich with plastic wrap. Remember or mark on the wrap which direction you want to cut the sandwich in half to show the beautiful cut section of the fruit.
8. Refrigerate for 1 hour or overnight. Then Remove the plastic wrap and gently cut in half each sandwich with a sharp knife. Cut the crusts off if you want.

Grilled Almond Butter, Dark Chocolate, & Pomegranate Sandwich

Ingredients

- 4 slices whole grain crusty bread
- 2 Tbsp dairy-free butter (such as olive oil)

- 4 Tbsp roasted salted almond butter
- 4 squares dark chocolate (dairy-free for vegan; don't exceed 70% cacao)
- 2-3 Tbsp pomegranate perils*

Instructions

1. Heat a large skillet over medium heat.
2. Butter the outsides of the slices of bread, then slather the inside of half of the slices with almond butter.
3. Next add 2 squares of chocolate on top of each of the almond butter slices and top with pomegranate arils. Top with the other slice of bread, buttered side up and place the sandwich in the skillet.
4. Push down with a heavy spatula to compress. Gently flip when the bottom is browned and crusty – about 2-3 minutes. (be careful not to burn)
5. Cook for another 2-3 minutes on the other side.

Grilled Mozzarella Sandwich

TO MAKE THE PESTO: Place the **basil, garlic, walnuts and Parmesan cheese in the food processor;** season with salt and pepper, to taste, and blend. While the food processor is on, pour the olive oil slowly into the mixture in order to allow the olive oil to emulsify.

For the Sandwich

- 4 slices sourdough bread
- 4 oz mozzarella cheese sliced
- 1 large tomato sliced
- 2 oz roasted red peppers jarred
- For the Pesto
- 1/2 cup fresh basil leaves
- 2 cloves garlic clove peeled
- 2 tablespoons walnuts
- 2 tablespoons grated Parmesan
- Salt and pepper
- 1/4 cup olive oil

INSTRUCTIONS

- To make the pesto, place the basil, garlic, walnuts and Parmesan cheese in the food processor; season with salt and pepper, to taste, and blend. While the food processor is on, pour the olive oil slowly into the mixture in order to allow the olive oil to emulsify.
- Spread the pesto equally on the 4 slices of bread and place two slices of bread on the sandwich maker or in a toaster oven for 2 minutes.
- Then place the mozzarella cheese, tomatoes and roasted red peppers on top of two bread slices and allow the cheese to melt and the veggies to soften, keeping the panini maker open.
- Once the cheese starts to melt, add the second slices on top to close the sandwiches, then close the panini maker for 2-3 minutes. Remove, slice in half and serve immediately

CUCUMBER SANDWICHES WITH CREAM CHEESE

Slice cucumber very thinly using a mandolin and if your knife skill is great, then use a knife but ensure that the cucumber slices are paper-thin.

Make the cream cheese filling. Start by adding the cream cheese and mayonnaise together into a bowl until smooth. Add dill and stir to combine. Finally, season with some salt and pepper adjusting to preference.

Assemble the sandwich, start by spreading the cream cheese filling on bread slices. Followed by the cucumber slices, layer it on the cream cheese spread and top it with another slice of bread. Using a sharp or serrated knife, cut off the crust if you haven't done this beforehand. Then cut the sandwich into 3 fingers.

Rajma Sandwich

Ingredients

- 1/2 cup boiled rajma
- 1 small onion finely chopped
- 1/2 green capsicum finely chopped
- 1/2 red bellpepper finely chopped
- 1 tsp chaat masala
- 1/2 tsp garam masala
- 1/2 tsp coriander powder
- Salt to taste
- Bread slices as required
- Oil for frying

Method

1. Mix all the ingredients except bread slices.
2. Cut the corners of bread and wet it with water slightly.

3. Put a little mixture on the bread slice.
4. Cover with another wet slice of bread.
5. Press the slices together,so that the filling does not comes out.
6. Prepare the other sandwiches like this.
7. Either deep fry or shallow fry them or cook them over a tawa (recommended)
8. Serve with dip of your choice.

ALOO SANDWICH

Preparing the aloo masala filling.

1. Rinse and scrub 2 large potatoes or 400 grams of potatoes well. Cut them into half and boil or steam or cook in an instant pot until they are completely cooked and soft.

Steam- for 10 minutes

Pressure cook- for 3 whistles

Instant pot- 6 minutes in pressure cooker or manual mode with pressure valve in seal position.

Along with potatoes also cook 1/2 cup shelled green peas if using.

Once done, peel and mash the boiled potatoes well. Set aside the mashed potato.

2. Heat a pan and add 2 teaspoons oil. Add 1/2 teaspoons cumin seeds and let it crackle.
3. Add peas and saute well for few minutes.
4. Add mashed potatoes and mix well. Add salt, turmeric powder, chaat masala powder, red chili powder and pepper powder. Saute and cook for 4-5 minutes. Add few drops of lemon juice. Mix well and switch off the flame. Remove to a bowl and set aside.
5. Take 4 bread slices and remove the edges.
6. Apply little oil or butter on all the slices.
7. Place 2-3 tablespoons of prepared potato filling on one slice and close with other slice. Repeat the same with 2 more bread slices.
8. Place the prepared bread on a preheated sandwich maker and toast till the sandwich turns crisp. You can alternately toast in a hot tava too. First toast until the base turns crispy and golden. Then flip and toast the other side.
9. Serve potato sandwich hot or cool slightly and pack in a tiffin.

Paneer Sandwich

Ingredients

- 2 slices of Sandwich bread
- 100 grams Paneer
- 1 small onion – chopped finely
- 1/4 Capsicum – chopped (you can use any color, I used green)
- 1 small Carrot, grated

- 1/4 tsp Garam masala
- A pinch of Turmeric
- Salt to taste
- 1-2 tsp Oil

Method

1. Crumble the paneer and keep it aside with the other ingredients.
2. In a pan or kadai, heat some oil and toss in the onions. Fry till translucent.
3. Add in the vegetables and fry for a couple of minutes, so that they are cooked but not too soft.
4. Add the masala powders and fry some more. Season to taste.
5. Add in the crumbled paneer and stir to mix well. Turn off the heat.
6. On a heated pan, place a slice of bread, add some paneer filling on top and cover with another slice. Alternatively, you can also use an electric grill.
7. Toast on both sides till light brown. Cut into triangles and serve with tomato ketchup.

Chutney Grilled Cheese

Ingredients

- 2 cups chopped bell peppers (1 Green Bell Pepper + 1 Red Bell Pepper)
- 1 tsp garam masala
- 2 tsp taco seasoning
- 1 tbsp oil
- 6-8 Pieces of Sandwich Bread
- 10-12 Slices of Cheese
- 1-2 tbsp butter

Spicy Mayo:

1/3 cup Hellman's Mayo

1/2 tsp Thecha Chutney (or Sriracha/Chili Garlic Sauce)

Cilantro Chutney:

- 1 large bunch cilantro, chopped roughly (only bottom 1 inch of stems removed)
- 4 large cloves garlic, peeled
- 1/2 inch piece ginger
- 3 Serrano Chilis or milder chilis like Jalapeño , roughly chopped
- 1 tsp cumin powder

- small handful of plain unsalted peanuts (or about 3 tbsp)
- 1/4 tsp salt *or to taste*
- water as needed

Place the above ingredients in a small blender or nutribullet until smooth. *Add 1-2 tbsp of water at a time as needed. The chutney should not be too watery so the grilled cheese doesn't become soggy.

Instructions

1. Heat a large skillet over medium high heat and oil. Once oil is hot, add the chopped bell peppers and cook for 3-4 minutes until slightly softened. (You want them to be soft but not mushy or watery at all. Cook the bell peppers on a high heat so they release less liquid (too much liquid in the peppers will make the grilled cheese soggy).
2. Once the bell peppers have cooked down a bit, add the taco seasoning & garam masala. Stir for about 2 minutes and then turn off the stove. Do not add salt (there is enough salt in the cheese, mayo, chutney etc).
3. In a large non stick skillet over medium heat, melt a few thin slices of butter and then add two slices of bread. Add one or two slices of cheese on one slice of bread.
4. On the other slice, spread a small amount of the spicy mayo, top with a slice of cheese (you can add more cheese, or stagger a few torn slices to make sure the entire slice of bread is covered) and then top with a spoonful of the bell peppers. Top the bell peppers with a spoon full of chutney and spread it evenly using the back of a spoon to make sure the peppers are all in an even layer.
5. Using a spatula slowly flip the other slice of bread on top and gently press down. Cook the grilled cheese over low heat until golden on both sides and until the cheese has melted.
6. Remove from pan

HOW TO MAKE AVOCADO SANDWICH

Wash and cut avocado into two. Remove the seed and scoop the pulp from the fruit.

Mash the pulp and add finely chopped onion, coriander leaves, lemon, green chilli and salt. Mix well.

Take 2 bread slices, apply butter on one and spread avocado mixture in the next slice.

Cover and toast in the sandwich maker or cook in dosa tawa greased with butter.

Cook both the sides. Remove and serve with tomato ketchup

Make A Healthy Sandwich

A slice of good bread and the fillings are what make a sandwich. That said, you cannot put just anything between two slices of bread and call it a sandwich. Similarly, not every bread that you choose can make a sandwich healthy. There are a few specific ones which rule this game.

So, here are some of the most popular and time-tested bread types and fillings for making a tasty sandwich for kids.

- The most basic bread types to make a sandwich healthy are whole wheat and multigrain bread. These are the versions that are well-known due to their acceptability and availability. But, the list does not end here. There is a lot more in the healthy bread bucket that you can try to enhance your sandwich's nutritional value. A few examples are sprouted whole grain bread, sourdough, sprouted rye bread, oats and flax bread to name a few.
- Cheese: You can try different varieties of cheese in a sandwich; cheese and dairy alternatives like tofu also taste good in a sandwich.
- Fruits including berries, green apple, pears, and grapes
- Nuts
- Veggies like beets, carrots, potato, corn, onion, tomato, lettuce, peppers and more

CHAPTER SEVEN

Healthy Waffle

Oat Waffles

These light, crispy-on-the-outside, fluffy-on-the-inside, gluten-free waffles are my favorite waffles! They're heart healthy, too. This waffle recipe requires just one flour, oat flour, which you can easily make yourself

INGREDIENTS

- 1 ½ cups (128 grams) oat flour, certified gluten-free if necessary
- 2 teaspoons baking powder
- ½ teaspoon salt
- Pinch of cinnamon, optional
- ¾ cup room temperature milk of choice (light coconut milk, nut milk, cow's milk)
- ¼ cup + 1 tablespoon melted coconut oil or 5 tablespoons unsalted butter, melted
- 2 tablespoons maple syrup
- 1 teaspoon vanilla extract

INSTRUCTIONS

1. In a mixing bowl, whisk together the dry ingredients: oat flour, baking powder, salt and cinnamon. In another bowl, whisk together the wet ingredients: milk, melted coconut oil or butter, maple syrup and vanilla extract. (If your coconut oil solidifies on contact with cold ingredients, gently heat the wet mixture in the microwave in ten seconds intervals, until it melts again.)
2. Pour the wet ingredients into the dry ingredients. Stir with a big spoon until just combined (the batter will still be a little lumpy). Let the batter rest for 10 minutes so the oat flour has time to soak up some of the moisture. Plug in your waffle iron to preheat now (if your waffle iron has a temperature/browning dial, set it to medium-high).
3. Once 10 minutes is up, give the batter one more swirl with your spoon. Pour batter onto the heated waffle iron, enough to cover the center and most of the central surface area, and close the lid. Once the waffle is deeply golden

and crisp, transfer it to a cooling rack or baking sheet. Don't stack your waffles on top of each other, or they'll lose crispness. If desired, keep your waffles warm by placing them in a 200 degree oven until you're ready to serve.

4. Repeat with remaining batter. Serve waffles with maple syrup and nut butter, or any other toppings that sound good!

Savoury Waffles

Savoury waffles loaded with vegetables. These Savoury Waffles recipe is perfect when you need a quick and healthy snack in minutes.

Ingredients

Since the base of this recipe is leftover Idli batter you need freshly prepared idli batter or leftover idli batter along with your choice of vegetables to make it healthier.

- Idli/dosa batter
- Purple cabbage
- Green chillies
- Zucchini
- Cilantro
- Salt
- Flex Seeds
- Olive Oil spray/olive oil

Instructions

- This recipe is super easy to cook. If your idli batter is prepared then it takes approximately 10 minutes to make complete batter, chop veggies and cook these waffles. Below is Step by step method with pictures.
- Mix together cabbage, leftover idli batter, green chillies, salt.
- Combine everything and make thick batter
- Also add grated zucchini and chopped coriander/cilantro leaves.
- Heat waffle press and spray with olive oil.
- Pour batter in the cavity of waffle press
- Cover and cook for 3-4 minutes
- Hint: For quick turnout of waffles make sure to preheat the waffle press for 2-3 minutes before pouring batter for the first batch. This step will also ensure that waffles do not stick to press and come out easily. In this recipe I have used this Lifeline waffle maker.

DOSA WAFFLES

INGREDIENTS

Dosa batter – preferably a day or two day old dosa batter.

Veggies – I used onion and carrot, you can also add tomato.

For heat – I added finely chopped green chili.

STEP BY STEP METHOD –

1- To a large bowl add the dosa batter which was already prepared.

2 & 3 – Add finely chopped onion, grated carrot, chopped coriander leaves and finely chopped green chili to the dosa batter. You can also add chopped ginger.

4- You may need to add a little bit of salt depending on how much salt your dosa batter. Mix all the ingredients. If the batter feels too thick, add 1 -2 tablespoons of water to it.

5- Preheat your waffle maker and spray it with oil. You can also brush it some oil.

6 – Preheat the waffle maker and spray some oil. To my round waffle maker I added about ¾th cup of the batter in the middle.Using a spatula spread the batter to fill the cavities and drizzle some oil (optional).

Cook the waffle as per instructions. You can select the desired level depending on your preference. It took me 4 minutes for the waffle to cook. Once done, gently remove the waffle with a spatula and serve it with chutney.

GREEN MOONG DAL WAFFLES

INGREDIENTS:

Green Moong Dal – use whole green moong dal

STEP BY STEP METHOD:

1- Wash and soak the green moong dal in plenty of water for 8 hours or overnight. After 8 hours, rinse the dal and drain the water completely.

2 – Add the dal to a blender. Add the green chili, ginger and cumin seeds.

3 – Add ¾th cup of water and grind the dal. It should be ground well but doesn't have to be super smooth.

4 – In a plate add finely chopped onion, grated carrot and chopped coriander. Mix it well.

5 – Transfer the batter to a large bowl and add the onion mixture.

6 – Add salt and mix the batter. If you feel the batter is too thick add some water, not too much. I added ¼th cup of water to the batter.

7 – Preheat the waffle maker and spray some oil. To my round waffle maker I added about ¾th cup of the batter in the middle.

8 – Using a spatula spread the batter to fill the cavities and drizzle some oil (optional).

9 – Cook the waffle as per instructions. You can select the desired level depending on your preference. It may take 3-4 minutes for the waffle to cook. Once done, gently remove the waffle with a spatula and serve it with chutney.

CHICKPEA FLOUR WAFFLES

These waffles are a fun play on the popular Indian snack. Light crispy waffles made with chickpea flour with plenty of veggie goodness and spices in them!

Ingredients

- ½ cup finely chopped cauliflower or use more onion or other seasonal veggie. Grate the veggie if they are not quick cooking eg sweet potato, root veg etc)
- ½ cup chopped bell pepper
- ¾ cup finely chopped onion
- 1 hot green chili finely chopped
- ½ inch of fresh ginger minced
- ¼ cup Or more cilantro chopped
- ⅛ tsp carom(ajwain) seeds or cumin seeds
- ½ tsp turmeric
- ¼ tsp cayenne or red Indian chili powder
- ½ tsp salt
- 2 Tbsp rice flour or use fine semolina flour
- 1 cup chickpea flour or use 1 cup +2 tbsp besan
- 1/8 tsp baking soda
- 1 cup water
- oil as needed

Instructions

1. Chop all of your vegetables and add them to a bowl. Or use a food processor to make a coarsely chopped mixture
2. Add the rice flour, chickpea flour, salt, spices, cilantro, baking soda and mix everything well.
3. Add in 1 cup of water to the mixture, stir well until combined. Add more water if needed - I need just about 1Tbsp more water when I make this, it really just depends on the amount of moisture leaking from your vegetables as well as the chickpea flour you use.
4. Let this mixture sit for 5 minutes before starting to make your waffles.
5. Oil and preheat your waffle maker - I usually drizzle some oil onto my waffle iron since I like my waffles to get nice and crispy and brown.
6. Pour and spread the thick batter on your waffle maker, spread evenly with a spatula. keep the batter amount to a medium thick layer for crispy waffles. Too thick will take long to cook and soften faster
7. Drizzle a few drops of oil on the top as well before closing the lid.

8. Cook until golden brown and crisp, to preference. (These waffles take a while to crisp up so account for all the inactive time when planning. Also keep them thin else the batter gets bready)
9. The waffle maker timer for mine is pretty short, you may have to experiment to see what's best for yours. Just make sure you cook it to a golden crisp brown to ensure the vegetables are fully cooked and the waffles get crispy.
10. Remove the waffle from the waffle maker, repeat for all of the batter.
11. These waffles are served best when they are warm and crispy, they will soften a bit as they cool off after about 30 mins or so.

Make Whole Wheat Eggless Waffles

Mix Dry ingredients

1. First pour 1 cup of whole wheat flour (or atta) into a mixing bowl.

2. Then add 1 pinch of salt.

Note: Skip adding salt if using salted butter.

3. Next add ¼ teaspoon of ground cinnamon powder.

If you are not a fan of cinnamon, then chose not to add it.

4. Then add 3 teaspoons of sugar.

Note: You can add more or less sugar depending on your taste preferences. You can even skip this step entirely if desired.

5. Now add 1 teaspoon of baking powder.

If possible use aluminium free baking powder.

6. Then use a wired whisk to mix all the dry ingredients very well. When fully combined, set aside.

7. Now preheat the waffle pan or waffle maker.

8. While the waffle iron preheats, pour 1¼-1¾ cups of milk in a saucepan. Keep the pan on a medium-low heat, then begin to the heat milk.

9. Stir occasionally while the milk heats. The milk should get hot for your eggless waffle batter, but do not let it boil.

10. When the milk becomes hot, add 1 tablespoon of unsalted butter.

11. Mix the butter in the hot milk very well.

12. Then add ½ teaspoon of vanilla extract.

13. Then mix well again.

14. Now pour the milk mixture into the dry ingredients.

15. Then with a wired whisk, begin to mix gently but well. Break apart the lumps with the whisk and make a smooth batter. A few tiny lumps are fine.

16. Make sure the eggless waffle batter is of a pourable consistency and not thick.

17. When the waffle pan or waffle maker becomes hot, spread some softened unsalted butter on it using a silicon brush.

18. Using a ⅓ to ½ measuring cup or a ladle, the pour the eggless waffle batter evenly on the waffle plates.

19. Close the waffle maker and cook for 7 to 8 minutes or more until the top looks crispy and golden.

20. When the waffles look crisp and golden, then open the waffle maker. Gently remove the eggless waffles with a wooden spatula.

Green peas waffle

NGREDIENTS

- 200 g buckwheat flour
- 200 g chickpea flour
- 250 g frozen peas
- 300 ml oat milk
- 4 tbsp tapioca flour
- 2 tsp baking powder
- salt & pepper to taste

For the topping:

- 1 avocado
- Half a cucumber
- Handful sprouts
- 1 lemon

INSTRUCTIONS

1. Add the peas and the oat milk to the blender and finely puree.
2. Mix buckwheat flour, chickpea flour, tapioca and baking powder in a bowl.
3. Add the pureed peas to the flour mixture and make a smooth, slightly liquid dough.
4. Pour some additional oat milk if necessary.
5. Season with salt and pepper.
6. Heat and grease the waffle iron.
7. Pour the dough into the waffle iron in batches.
8. Remove the slightly brown waffles with a fork and place them next to each other on a cooling rack.
9. Served them with avocado, cucumber, sprouts and lemon!

Best Waffle Toppings

Whipped Cream: Whipped cream is a classic topping for desserts, but it goes great on waffles as well.

If you've ever ordered waffles at a restaurant, they're likely to serve them to you with a dollop of whipped cream on top.

You can replicate this presentation at home and on top of virtually any sweet waffle with a dollop (or more) of whipped cream.

Whether you prefer store-bought whipped cream or you like to make your own, this classic whipped topping goes particularly well with fruit toppings like peaches and strawberries.

If you're a waffle connoisseur, you can put fruit directly into your waffle batter instead of as a topping, and then the only thing you need to complete your waffle is a dollop of whipped cream!

Maple Syrup : Perhaps the most classic waffle topping, there was no way I could write an article about waffle toppings and not mention maple syrup.

Whether you like table syrup or pure maple syrup, plain waffles with syrup are a classic combination, and sometimes it feels good to get back to the basics.

Best of all? Both table syrup and pure maple syrup have a long shelf life, so even if you feel like the initial investment is costly (in the case of pure maple syrup), it will last for a long time, so you can keep coming back to this treat over and over again.

Cinnamon Sugar: A classic topping for any breakfast treat and especially popular amongst kids, cinnamon sugar is an excellent addition to any waffle.

You can easily combine it with other toppings like bananas and whipped cream.

Store-bought cinnamon sugar is a staple in many pantries, but don't panic if you're out; you can make it at home with the same two ingredients in its name: cinnamon and sugar.

To make, simply pour some white sugar into a bowl, using a fork to break up any chunks that have formed. Next, pour in the desired amount of cinnamon (start with a few dashes and work up from there) and mix.

Store any leftover cinnamon sugar you have for next time, or pour it straight into your waffle batter to spice things up!

Bananas: Bananas are another classic waffle topping, and they're a great addition if you're looking to make your waffles a little healthier.

Bananas are naturally sweet, so this calcium and potassium-rich food is an excellent option if you're trying to avoid adding sugar; pair bananas with peanut butter for a healthy sweet and salty breakfast option.

You can also chop fresh nuts like walnuts or pecans and sprinkle them on your waffles with bananas. Finally, add cinnamon sugar for a little extra sweetness.

If you're not afraid of an ultra-sweet breakfast, bananas are great on top of waffles when paired with Nutella or honey.

Peaches: Fresh peaches are one of the best things about summer, and desserts like peach cobbler can be modified and turned into a breakfast treat if you have the time.

For the ultimate waffle experience, try cooking fresh peaches and making a crumble, then serve these on top of your waffles and top it all off with some whipped cream.

A pared-down version of this lavish breakfast can be made year-round with store-bought canned peaches as well!

Simply heat the peaches on the stovetop or in a microwave-safe bowl, and pour them on top of your waffles. Add a little whipped cream and chopped nuts for extra sweetness and crunch, if you want.

Don't be afraid to pour some of the peach juice on the waffles; it soaks in and tastes extra yummy!

Strawberries: Strawberries are one of the most classic waffle toppings, and with good reason.

This delicious fruit is so sweet and fresh tasting that it perfectly complements waffles.

If you have fresh strawberries on hand, there are a few ways you can prepare them as a waffle topping; first, simply chop them up into bite-sized pieces and place them on top of your waffles, topping it all off with a dollop of whipped cream.

If you prefer sweeter waffle toppings, you can chop your strawberries up, put them in a bowl, and pour a tablespoon or two of white sugar on top.

Mix the strawberries and sugar until they get a little juicy, and leave them in the bowl until you're ready to serve your waffles.

Stir the strawberry sugar mixture one last time and drizzle the strawberries over your waffles!

You can also make it easy on yourself and just get storebought strawberry topping to keep in your fridge whenever you make waffles.

Honey: Honey is the perfect topping if you want to add a little sweetness to your waffles, but you're not a huge maple syrup fan.

Honey is a relatively healthy sweetener, and it goes well with a variety of sweet and savory toppings.

You can add honey to waffles that have bananas, nuts, or peanut butter on them if you want a sweet treat for breakfast, or you can even drizzle a fried chicken waffle in honey for a sweet kick.

Peanut Butter: Peanut butter is a perfect topping for anyone looking to add a little protein to their waffle breakfast. You can use peanut butter as the only topping for your waffles or add other items like honey or Nutella to add a little sweetness to your breakfast.

Consider peanut butter, chopped nuts, and sliced banana as waffle toppings for a delicious but healthy breakfast if you're trying to eat better. If you or someone you know is allergic to peanut butter, numerous nut butter substitutes are available, including almond butter and sunflower butter.

Chocolate Chips: Even if you're a fully-fledged adult, you can't escape the joy of chocolate chips on your waffles. Chocolate chips make great toppings on waffles and are incredibly delicious when added to the batter and cooked.

Although I added chocolate chips as a topping, I personally prefer them added to the waffle batter because the chocolate chips melt in the waffle iron and seep into the batter. You can then top the waffle with anything else, from maple syrup to powdered sugar and bananas. If you're looking for a particularly decadent treat, add chocolate chips to your waffle batter and then top the whole thing off with Nutella.

Nutella : Nutella is a classic addition to crepes, a delicious French breakfast, so it stands to reason that it would be just as good on top of waffles. Nutella is a chocolate-hazelnut spread, and it goes great on its own or combined with other waffle toppings. An absolute favorite combination of mine is Nutella, sliced bananas, and chopped nuts, but you can enjoy Nutella on your waffles in whatever way you like most!

Blueberries : Blueberries are almost as classic of a waffle topping as strawberries, and you can enjoy this summery fruit in numerous ways.

Pour fresh blueberries directly onto your waffles and then top with whipped cream for a simple and fresh-tasting breakfast, or cook your blueberries down into a berry compote.

Berry compotes make great waffle toppings because you get the sweet berry flavor of the fruit with an almost syrup-like consistency.

Try store-bought blueberry syrup if you want to keep it simple and have an excellent blueberry topping on hand year-round.

Cherries : The final topping on this list might not be something you've had on your waffles before, but I assure you, it's delicious. If you have an abundance of fresh cherries around the house, you can chop them into small pieces and mix them into your waffle batter to cook them in the waffles.

You can also prepare them like fresh strawberries and mix the fresh fruit with white sugar to bring out their natural sweetness. But there's no need to complicate it if it's not cherry season! Instead, consider buying cherry pie filling from the store and topping your waffles off with whipped cream.

Best Waffle Toppings

- Whipped Cream
- Maple Syrup
- Cinnamon Sugar
- Ice Cream
- Bananas
- Peaches
- Strawberries
- Honey
- Peanut Butter
- Fried Eggs
- Fried Chicken
- Chocolate Chips
- Nutella
- Blueberries
- Cherries

CHAPTER EIGHT

Upma & Poha

RICE WITH MOONG DAL UPMA

NGREDIENTS

- 1 Cup Raw Rice Use Ponni / Sona Masoori / Basmati Rice
- ½ Cup Moong dal 1 Cup - 250ml. I
- 3¾ Cup Water 1 portion of Rice+Moong dal = 1.5 portion of water
- 1½ tsp Salt adjust to your taste
- FOR TEMPERING
- 1 tbsp Coconut Oil
- 1 tsp Mustard seeds
- 1 tsp Split Urad Dal
- 1 tbsp Split Bengal Gram (Channa Dal / Kadalaparuppu)
- 1 Pinch Asafoetida (Asafetida / Hing)
- 4 nos Red Chili Adjust to your spice level
- 1 sprig Curry Leaves
- 3 tbsp Grated Coconut optional

INSTRUCTIONS

DRY ROASTING

- Heat a pan. Add moong dal and dry roast in the low flame till you get a nice aroma. When the dal starts to change the color, then remove the dal from flame and set aside.
- In the same pan, add the rice. Dry roast the rice till the rice starts to change color slightly. Set this fried rice aside.

TEMPERING

- Heat oil in a pressure cooker. Add mustard seeds and allow the seeds to crackle.
- To the pressure cooker, add split urad dal and split bengal gram dal. Sauté the dal till the dal turns light brown.
- Next, tear the red chili and add it. Also, add curry leaves and hing. Give everything a good mix.
- Now, add the dry roasted moong dal and rice. Stir well so it gets mixed with the tempering.

COOKING UPMA

- Add 3¾ cup of water to the pressure cooker. Add salt. Stir well. (Note - 1 portion of Rice + Moongdal = 1.5 portion water)
- Close the pressure cooker and secure the whistle. Allow the usili upma to get pressure cooked for 2-3 whistles. (always cook 1 whistle less than what you usually cook for rice)
- Allow the pressure to naturally release. Open the pressure cooker and gently give a mix without breaking the rice.
- Finally add the grated coconut and give it a nice mix.
- Usili Upma is now ready to serve with Chutney.

Kanchipuram Rava Upma

INGREDIENTS

- cup Semolina (Sooji / Rava) 1 Cup - 250ml
- 1 tsp Ginger finely chopped
- 2 nos Green Chili adjust to your spice level
- 1 nos Onion
- 3 tbsp Grated Coconut
- 2 cups Water 1 portion of Rava = 2 portion of water
- 1 tsp Salt (adjust to your taste)

FOR TEMPERING

- 1 tbsp Oil
- 1 tsp Mustard seeds
- 1 tsp Split Urad Dal
- 1 tsp Peppercorns
- 1 tsp Cumin Seeds
- 1 sprig Curry leaves

INSTRUCTIONS

PREPARATION

- Heat the pan and add Rava (Sooji). Roast it till we get nice aroma from the Rava. Don't let the color of the rava change. It may take about 2-3 minuts. Keep the roasted rava aside.
- Peel the onion and chop it to small pieces. Also chop the green chillies and ginger and keep it aside.

TEMPERING

- Heat the oil (or ghee) in a pan. Add pepper and allow it to sputter. Then add the mustard seeds and cumin seeds. When the mustard seeds begins to sputter add the split urad dal. Fry them till the color of the dal change to golden brown.
- Now add the chopped onions, green chillies, ginger and curry leaves and saute the onions till they turn transparent.
- Add 2 tablespoon of coconut and add it to the pan of seasoned ingredients and fry it till it turns golden brown color.

MAKING UPMA

- Add water to the pan along with salt and allow it to boil. (Water to Rava Ratio - 1 portion of Rava = 2 portions of water).
- When the water starts to boil, add rava and stir it to finely so that the rava is cooked properly. You need to be very careful when adding the rava as it becomes round balls while adding in the hot water. To avoid this keep stirring the water and add the rava slowly and continuously.
- Once the water is absorbed, simmer the flame, cover the pan and cook the upma for about 3-5 minutes in low flame. Then finally add remaining coconut and mix well and remove from flame.
- The delicious Kanchipuram Rava uppuma is ready to serve.

PULIMA UPMA

INGREDIENTS

- 2 Cups Raw Rice We can use Ponni or Sona Masoori or Basmati
- 1 Gooseberry Size Tamarind Soak in 2.5 Cups of water & Extract the juice
- ¼ tsp Asafoetida (Asafetida / Hing)
- ¼ tsp Turmeric Powder

- Few Curry Leaves
- 2 Cups Water
- 2 tbsp Sesame Oil
- Salt As Needed

FOR TEMPERING

- 3 tbsp Sesame Oil
- 1 tsp Mustard Seeds
- 1 tsp Split Urad Dal
- 3 tsp Split Bengal Gram (Channa Dal / Kadalaparuppu)
- 1 tbsp Peanuts
- 5 Red Chili

INSTRUCTIONS

Soak tamarind in 2.5 cups of warm water and extract the juice

RICE RAVA PREPRATION

- Take 2 cups of rice. Sprinkle water to damp the rice. The rice should be just wet. Do not soak rice in water.
- Set the wet rice aside for about 10 mins to dry completely.
- Split the dried rice into two parts. Take one part to mixer jar and give a pulse or two. The rice should be broken but not be ground to powder. The consistency of the rice rava should be more coarse than the sooji we use for upma
- Repeat the same grinding process for the second part of the rice.

TEMPERING PROCESS

- Heat Sesame oil in a heavy bottomed pan. Add mustard seeds and allow it to sputter. Add split urad dal, bengal gram (kadalaparuppu) and peanuts and fry till dal turns golden brown.
- Then add hing, broken red chili, turmeric powder and curry leaves and saute for few seconds
- Add tamarind extract and water to the pan. Add salt and bring the tamarind water to boil
- When the water starts rolling boil, add the rice rava and keep stirring so that there are no lumps
- Cover & Cook the rice rava in medium flame. Open and stir in regular intervals to check if the rice is cooked and also to prevent burning or sticking to the bottom of the pan

- If the rice is not cooked completely but the tamarind water is fully absorbed, then add plain water and keep cooking the rice rava. Also if we add more water, we need to adjust the spice and salt. We can add red chili powder and also adjust salt.
- Once all rice rava is cooked completely and water is fully absorbed, switch off the flame. Close the pan with lid and let the upma remain aside for about 5-10 mins. This will make the upma to crumble a little.
- Serve the delicious Upma

IDLI UPMA

INGREDIENTS

- 10 nos Idli preferably leftover Idli
- 1 nos Onion Big Size
- 2 tsp Red Chili Powder (or) Idli Milagai Powder
- ¼ tsp Turmeric Powder
- ½ tsp Salt adust to your taste
- FOR TEMPERING
- 1 tsp Cooking Oil
- 1 tsp Mustard seeds
- ½ tsp Split Urad Dal
- ½ tsp Split Bengal Gram (Channa Dal / Kadalaparuppu)
- 1 handful Curry leaves
- 1 nos Green Chili

INSTRUCTIONS

PREPARATION

For Idli Upma, we need left over idlis which are not hot. Take the left over idlis and crumble them and keep it aside.

Finely chop the onion and green chilli and keep it aside.

START MAKING UPMA

- Heat oil in a pan, and add mustard seeds. When the mustard seeds starts to sputter, add urdhal and channa dal and fry till it turns brown color.
- To this add chopped green chilli and curry leaves and fry for 10 seconds. Then add chopped onions with a pinch of salt and saute the onions till it turns transparent.
- Add turmeric powder to the sauted onions. Now add the idly crumble and mix gently.

- Also add Idli Milagai Podi (or Red chili Powder) and toss them well so that the spice powder gets nicely coated to the cooked idlis. Adjust the salt and keep the idli upma in flame for 5 minutes and then switch off the flame
- Serve hot with chutney and enjoy the dish!

MULTIGRAIN BREAD UPMA

INGREDIENTS

- 6 Slices Bread
- 1 Onion Finely Chopped
- 1 Tomato Chopped
- ½ tsp Turmeric Powder
- 1 tsp Salt
- ¼ Cup Green Peas 1 Cup = 250ml
- 1 tbsp Coriander Leaves
- 1 tbsp Ghee
- ½ tsp Red Chili Powder
- FOR TEMPERING
- 1 tbsp Oil
- 1 tsp Mustard seeds
- 1 tsp Split Bengal Gram (Channa Dal / Kadalaparuppu)
- 1 Green Chili
- 1 sprig Curry Leaves
- 1 inch Ginger finely chopped

INSTRUCTIONS

PREPARATION

Finely chop the onions and tomatoes separately and keep it aside.

FRY BREAD CUBES

Cut the bread slices into diamond size pieces (or small square). Heat ghee in a pan and add the bread slices and fry it till it is crisp. Take the fried bread crumbs in a separate plate. (Alternateively you can skip this step and take the sliced bread directly to make the upma)

TEMPERING PROCESS

Heat oil in a pan. Add mustard seeds when the oil is hot. When the mustard seeds starts to sputter, add Bengal gram dal, curry leaves and fry till the urdal turns golden brown color.

MAKING UPMA

- Now add the chopped ginger, chopped green chillies and fry for few seconds. Add the chopped onions and fry till the onions turns transparent.
- Add the tomatoes, peas, salt, red chili powder, turmeric powder and fry them in medium flame. If required add 2-3 tablespoon of water to cook the peas. Cook until the mixture turns thick. Check the spice and salt and adjust it if required.
- Add the fried bread pieces and mix well. Allow the bread upma to cook for 2-3 minutes in low flame.
- Finally garnish with Coriander Leaves. Remove from flame. The yummy bread upma is serve hot!
- We can crush peanuts and add it to the upma. Also we can fry the cashews in ghee and add it to the mixture
- Enrich the bread umpa with mixed vegetables

Chappati Upma

Ingredients:

- Carrot 1
- Potato 1
- Beans 100gms
- Onion 1
- Tomato 1
- Chapatti 4
- Green Chilli 1
- Salt To Taste
- **For seasoning:**
- Oil 1 tablespoon
- Mustard seeds 1 teaspoon

Method:

- Cut the Chapattis into small pieces and keep it aside
- Chop the vegetables & onions into smaller pieces and keep it aside
- Heat the oil in pan, and add the mustard seeds. When the mustard seeds begins to sputter, add the broken chilli and chopped onion and fry till onion turns transparent
- Now add the chopped vegetables and fry them till they are cooked completely
- To these cooked vegetables, add chapatti pieces and mix it well. Add the necessary salt and mix it well
- Now the delicious Chapatti upma is ready to serve hot.
- You can also add Capsicum and Green Peas with this upma.

Ragi Pachchai Maa Puli Upma

Ingredients

For the upma batter

- 1 cup Ragi Flour (Finger Millet/ Nagli)
- 1 cup Curd (Dahi / Yogurt) , beaten
- Salt , as required

For seasoning

- 1/2 teaspoon Mustard seeds (Rai/ Kadugu)
- 1 teaspoon White Urad Dal (Split)
- Asafoetida (hing) , a pinch
- 3 Green Chillies , chopped
- 1/2 inch Ginger , chopped
- 1 teaspoon Curry leaves , chopped
- 4 tablespoons Ghee
- 1 teaspoon Curry leaves , chopped
- Oil , as required for seasoning and making the upma

How to make Ragi Pachchai Maa Puli Upma Recipe - Ragi Flour Upma Recipe

1. To begin making the Ragi Pachchai Maa Puli Upma recipe, make a thick batter out of ragi flour, salt and beaten curd in a bowl.
2. The consistency of the batter should be that of an idli batter. If needed add little water to get the thick pouring consistency. You will need approximately 3/4 to 1 cup of water.
3. Heat a pan/kadai and add ghee. Do the tempering of mustard, urad dal, green chillies, ginger, asafoetida and curry leaves. Allow the urad dal to turn golden brown and crisp.
4. Transfer the Ragi Pachchai Maa Puli Upma batter to the pan with the tempering and cook till it absorbs all the moisture and becomes grainy and little crispy. Cook on medium heat. It takes about 3 to 4 minutes for it to become grainy and cooked.
5. If you feel the Ragi Puli Upma is too dry, you can sprinkle some water and cook it further. Keep the pan covered and mix a couple of times in between and serve the Pachchai Maa Puli Upma immediately.
6. Serve the Pachchai Maa Puli Upma

Moong Dal Upma

Ingredients

- 1 cup Yellow Moong Dal (Split) , soaked for minimum 4 hours
- 2 Onions , finely chopped
- 10 Green Chillies , (adjust)
- 1/4 teaspoon Asafoetida (hing)
- 2 tablespoons Coriander (Dhania) Leaves , chopped
- 1/3 cup Green peas (Matar) , boiled
- 3 Dry Red Chillies
- 1 teaspoon Mustard seeds (Rai/ Kadugu)
- 2 teaspoons White Urad Dal (Split)
- 1 tablespoon Chana dal (Bengal Gram Dal)
- 1/2 Turmeric powder (Haldi)
- 50 grams Cashew nuts
- 1-1/2 teaspoons Enos Fruit Salt
- 1 Lemon , freshly squeezed
- 1 inch Ginger , chopped
- Oil , as needed
- Salt , to taste
- 2 tablespoons Fresh coconut , grated

How to make Moong Dal Upma

1. To begin making the upma,soak the moong dal for at least 4 hours. We need to get the moong dal mixture ready and preheat the steamer.
2. Preheat the Steamer/Idli steamer by bringing the water to a boil. Grease the idli plates.
3. In a mixer grinder, combine the soaked and drained moong dal, hing, green chillies, juice of half lemon, 1 tablespoon oil, salt, 3/4 cup of water and blend to a smooth paste.
4. Into a mixing bowl, add eno in 2 tablespoons of water and gently incorporate the ground moong dal without overworking. Ladle this moong dal batter into the idli plate and steam this for 20 minutes. It should be done in 20 minutes on medium high flame.
5. Turn off the flame. Remove the idli plates from the steamer and let this cool completely.
6. Once cooled completely, crumble the steamed moong dal cakes in a mixing bowl with your fingers and set aside.
7. In a large pan, heat some oil on medium flame, add mustard seeds to let it splutter

8. Now lower the heat and add urad dal, chana dal, hing, and cashews and ginger.
9. Keep stirring until they change colour, add curry leaves and add green and red chillies, allowing them to crackle.
10. Next add the onions and a pinch of salt and cook for 3-4 minutes until the onions are well cooked.
11. Add turmeric powder, boiled peas and stir. finally add in the crumbled steamed moong dal cakes and mix everything gently.
12. Add the juice from 1/2 a lemon and adjust salt. Combine and cook for maximum 2-3 minutes only, covered on low heat, until everything comes together.
13. Top Moong Dal Upma with coriander, freshly grated coconut.

Quinoa Vegetable Upma

Ingredients

- 1 cup Quinoa
- 2 cups Water
- 2 tablespoons Extra Virgin Olive Oil
- 1 teaspoon Mustard seeds (Rai/ Kadugu)
- 1/2 teaspoon Cumin seeds (Jeera)
- 1 teaspoon White Urad Dal (Split)
- 1 teaspoon Chana dal (Bengal Gram Dal)
- 6 Curry leaves
- 2 Green Chillies , finely chopped
- 1 Shallot , finely chopped
- 1 Tomato , finely chopped
- 1/4 cup Carrot (Gajjar) , finely chopped
- 1/4 Whole Corn Kernels
- 1/4 Green peas (Matar)
- Green beans (French Beans) , finely chopped
- 1/2 teaspoon Coriander Powder (Dhania)
- 1/2 teaspoon Garam masala powder
- Salt , as needed
- Coriander (Dhania) Leaves , few, chopped

How to make Quinoa Vegetable Upma Recipe

1. To begin making Quinoa Vegetable Khichdi, first heat a heavy bottomed pan on medium flame, add the olive oil and mustard seeds and allow them to splutter. Next add the cumin seeds, urad dal, channa dal, curry leaves and green chili. Saute it all for a few seconds.
2. Add the chopped shallots and sprinkle a little salt. Saute gently until they turn translucent. Next, add the vegetables - beans, carrots, corn, peas and cook on a medium flame until they are half cooked.
3. Next, add the chopped tomatoes, mix well and saute sauté for a couple of minutes. Follow this by adding coriander powder, garam masala, quinoa and sauté once again for a couple of minutes, until the masalas cook through.
4. Add 2 cups of water and adjust salt according to your taste.
5. Increase the heat to medium and bring the water to a boil. Then, reduce the heat and cover the pan, allowing the quinoa to cooked completely. It will absorb all the water completely.
6. Take the pan off the heat, garnish the Quinoa Vegetable Upma with fresh chopped coriander leaves and serve.

Foxtail Millet Upma

Ingredients

- 1 teaspoon Sesame (Gingelly) Oil
- 1/4 teaspoon Mustard seeds (Rai/ Kadugu)
- 1 teaspoon White Urad Dal (Split)
- 2 sprig Curry leaves , finely chopped
- 1 Green Chilli
- 1 Dry Red Chilli
- 1/2 cup Onion , finely chopped
- 1 inch Ginger , finely chopped
- 1/4 teaspoon Turmeric powder (Haldi)
- 1/4 cup Carrot (Gajjar) , finely chopped
- 1/4 cup Green beans , finely chopped
- 1 cup Foxtail Millet
- 1 Lemon , salt to taste
- 2 tablespoons Coriander (Dhania) Leaves , juice from one lemon
- 1 tablespoon Ghee

How to make Foxtail Millet Upma Recipe

1. To begin making the Foxtail Millet Upma, heat oil in a pressure cooker over medium heat; add mustard seeds and split urad dal and allow it to crackle. Allow the urad dal to turn golden brown and crisp.

2. Once the dal is golden brown, add the green chilli and red chilli and saute for a few seconds.
3. Add the onion, ginger and saute until the onions soften. Once the onion softens, add the curry leaves, turmeric powder, beans, carrots, foxtail millet, salt and 2-1/2 cups of water.
4. Cover the pressure cooker and pressure cook the millet upma for 5 to 6 whistles and simmer for 5 minutes and turn off the heat. Allow the pressure to release naturally
5. Once the pressure releases, give it a gentle stir. Squeeze in the juice from one lemon and stir in the chopped coriander leaves.
6. Serve Foxtail Millet Upma

Broken Barley Upma

Ingredients

- 1/2 cup Barley (seeds) , (Broken Barley)
- 1-1/2 Cups Water
- 1 Onion , finely chopped
- 1 teaspoon Ginger , grated
- 2 Green Chillies , finely chopped
- 1/2 cup Carrot (Gajjar) , diced small
- 1/2 cup Green beans (French Beans) , finely chopped
- 1/4 cup Green peas (Matar) , steamed
- 1 Tomato , chopped
- 2 tablespoon Raw Peanuts (Moongphali)
- 1 teaspoon Mustard seeds (Rai/ Kadugu)
- 1 tablespoon White Urad Dal (Split)
- 1 sprig Curry leaves , roughly chopped
- Salt , to taste
- 2 teaspoons Lemon juice
- Coriander (Dhania) Leaves , small bunch, chopped
- Oil , for cooking

How to make Broken Barley Upma Recipe

1. To make the Broken Barley Upma Recipe, heat the oil in a pressure cooker or a pan on medium heat, add the mustard seeds and allow it to crackle. Once it crackles add in the split urad dal and peanuts. Saute for a few minutes until the dal gets roasted.

2. Once roasted add chopped onions, ginger, green chilies, curry leaves and saute till onion turns translucent.
3. Add carrots, beans, peas and let it all cook for a minute or two stirring in between.
4. Now add barley grits mix well and saute for few minutes. Keep stirring else barley may stick to the cookers /pan's bottom.
5. Pour in the 1 cup of water. Stir in the salt and tomatoes and give the mixture a good stir.
6. Cover the pressure cook for 2 whistles. Turn off the flame and allow the pressure to release naturally.
7. Once the pressure has released, open the cooker, add the lemon juice and coriander leaves. Mix well and serve hot.

Broken Wheat Upma

Ingredients

- 1 cup Broken Wheat
- 1 tbsp Oil
- 1/2 tbsp Ghee
- 1/4 tsp Mustard Seeds
- 1/4 tsp Cumin Seeds
- 1/2 " inch Cinnamon Stick
- 2 Cloves
- A sprig of Curry Leaves
- 1 tsp Ginger finely chopped
- 2 Green Chillies
- 1/2 cup Onion finely chopped
- 2 tbsp Chopped Carrots (optional)
- 2 tbsp Green Peas (optional)
- 1/4 cup Tomato finely chopped
- 1/8 tsp Turmeric Powder
- 2 cups of Water
- Salt as required

Directions

- Firstly, roast 1 cup of broken wheat until it's roasted and its color changes.
- Once roasted remove from the flame & allow it to cool down.
- Once cooled wash and clean the broken wheat. Drain it & keep it aside.

- Now heat 2 tbsp oil and 1/2 tbsp ghee in a pan.
- Crackle 1/4 tsp mustard seeds. Followed by 1/4 tsp Cumin Seeds, 1/2 " inch Cinnamon Stick, 2 Cloves, a sprig of Curry Leaves, 1 tsp Ginger (Chopped), and 2 Green Chilies. Saute them until it is roasted and the raw smell of ginger disappears.
- Now saute 1/2 cup of finely chopped onion and 1/8 tsp or 2 pinches of turmeric powder.
- Then add in 2 tbsp chopped carrots and 2 tbsp green peas and saute them for 2 minutes.
- Now add 1/4 cup of finely chopped tomatoes and saute them again for 3 minutes.
- Add 2 cups of hot water or normal water and salt as required. Cover and bring this to boil.
- Once it starts to boil add the broken wheat. Mix it well. Cover and cook for about 20 minutes over low flame.
- Stir in between & check if there is water. After 20 minutes, the water is completely absorbed by wheat and is cooked well.
- Broken wheat upma is ready to serve.

Semiya Upma

Ingredients

- 1 cup Semiya/vermicelli
- 2 tsp+3tsp oil
- Salt as required
- 1/2 tsp mustard seeds
- 1/2 tsp urad dal
- 1/2 tsp chana dal
- 2 red chilli
- Fresh curry leaves
- 1 tbsp Finely chopped ginger
- 2 ½ cup water
- 1 green chilly finely chopped
- 2 tbsp chopped carrots
- 2 tbsp cooked green peas
- 2 tbsp chopped beans
- 1/4 tsp turmeric powder
- 1/2 tbsp lemon juice

Directions

- **Roasting semiya**
- For that add 2tsp oil in a pan , followed by 1cup vermicelli.
- Roast it over the low-medium flame by stirring continuously till it turns to a golden brown. (If you have roasted vermicelli you can avoid this step)
- **Cooking semiya**
- Let us cook vermicelli now. In a pan add some water along with 1/2tsp salt. Once it starts to boil add in the roasted vermicelli. (If you have not used oil while roasting vermicelli now you can add 1tsp oil along with hot water to avoid stickiness)
- Close the pan & boil for 3min. Once cooked strain the water & keep vermicelli aside.
- **Preparing Semiya Upma**
- Add 1 tsp oil in a preheated pan. Add in 1/2 tsp mustard seeds, 1/2 tsp urad dal & 1/2 tsp chana dal. When mustard seeds starts to splutter add fresh curry leaves, dried red chilly, chopped ginger & chopped green chilly.
- Saute till ginger turns golden color. Now add in 2 tbsp onion, 2 tbsp carrots, 2 tbsp green peas, 2 tbsp beans.
- Saute for 1 min over high flame. Then add in 1/4 tsp turmeric powder & salt as required. Saute for 2 min.
- Add cooked semiya & mix well for 2 min.
- Our semiya upma is ready to be served.
- For a nice flavor add 1/2 tbsp lemon juice (optional) before serving.

Notes

- If you have not used oil while roasting vermicelli you can add 1tsp oil along with hot water to avoid stickiness.

Poha

Most of us prepare *poha* is by adding moistened *chivda* to sauteed spices, onions, peanuts and *haldi*. While this is the basic procedure of preparing the dish, there are many versatile ways in which *poha* is prepared in different parts of India.

To make the poha dish, beaten rice is first lightly washed in water allowing it to sit for a few minutes before it is cooked, tempered, mashed according to what pleases your palette. In different regions of our country poha is cooked differently, drawing influences from that region's locally available ingredients, commonly used spices, taste preferences, cooking techniques etc.

Variants Tadka: you can add paanch fodan , Saunf , Ajwain , Hing based on your taste buds

Vegetables: you can add tomato, potato , mix vegetables , leafy vegetables , cottage cheese , soya chunks

Nuts: you can add peanuts , mix nuts , or your favourite

Commitments: Chana/ green peas Spicy Curry, Allo Sev, Ratlami Sev , Chopped Kachumber

Type Of Poha : Ragi Poha / Red Rice Poha / Regular Poha

CHAPTER NINE

Idli and chutnies

You can use mini or button idli sacha for making idli

Mint Peanut Chutney

Ingredients

- roasted peanuts/groundnut
- mint/pudina
- cilantro/coriander leaves
- onion
- green chilies/red chilies
- jeera seeds (cumin)
- tamarind optional
- garlic cloves
- oil
- salt to taste

How to make Mint Peanut Chutney

- Roast peanuts in a pan on medium flame until golden brown. Remove and let it cool down.
- In a pan, add oil, jeera, onion/shallots, green chili, garlic, and saute well till onions turn brown. It roughly takes 2-3 minutes.
- Then add mint, coriander leaves, and tamarind saute for 1 minute (till the mint leaves shrink), and turn off the heat. Cool completely.
- In a blender jar, add roasted peanuts, mint mixture, salt, water, and blend to a coarse or smooth paste as per your preference.

Coconut Chutney (Nariyal Chutney)

Ingredients

- **Coconut** - Freshly grated coconut works best for this chutney. However, you can also use frozen coconut or unsweetened desiccated coconut flakes.
- **Ginger** - use fresh ginger for the best flavor.
- **Green Chili** - I used one Thai green chili for the heat, you can increase or decrease it according to your preference.
- **Roasted chana dal(Fried gram)** - also known as Dalia in Hindi, adds great texture to the chutney, so don't skip it. If you don't have it, you can substitute it with cashews, or roasted peanuts.
- **Tamarind** - Adds tanginess to the nariyal chutney. You can also use store-bought tamarind paste if that is what you have in hand. You may also substitute it with lemon juice or yogurt.
- **Tempering** - mustard seeds, urad dal, curry leaves, red chili, and oil are used for this tempering.

Why You'll Love this Coconut Chutney

- Easy to make and ready in 10 minutes.
- Uses simple and basic pantry ingredients.
- The perfect accompaniment to idli, dosa, medu vada, and more.
- Tastes better than the one you get at the restaurants.
- It is vegan, nut-free, and can be made gluten-free by skipping asafoetida.

Ingredients for making White Coconut Chutney

- **Coconut** - Freshly grated coconut works best for this chutney. However, you can also use frozen coconut or unsweetened desiccated coconut flakes.
- **Ginger** - use fresh ginger for the best flavor.
- **Green Chili** - I used one Thai green chili for the heat, you can increase or decrease it according to your preference.
- **Roasted chana dal(Fried gram)** - also known as Dalia in Hindi, adds great texture to the chutney, so don't skip it. If you don't have it, you can substitute it with cashews, or roasted peanuts.
- **Tamarind** - Adds tanginess to the nariyal chutney. You can also use store-bought tamarind paste if that is what you have in hand. You may also substitute it with lemon juice or yogurt.
- **Tempering** - mustard seeds, urad dal, curry leaves, red chili, and oil are used for this tempering.

How to Make Coconut Chutney

Add fresh coconut, green chilies, ginger, tamarind, salt, and water into a mixer grinder jar. Blend to a smooth paste. Add extra water as needed to get the desired consistency.

For Tempering

- Heat coconut oil in a small pan, add mustard seeds, urad dal, and dry red chili, and fry till the dal turns light brown.
- Then add curry leaves and hing. Saute for a few seconds and pour the tempering over the ground chutney.

Make the Best Coconut Chutney

- **Use fresh coconut:** Freshly grated coconut gives the best flavor and texture to this nariyal chutney recipe, but you may also use frozen coconut or desiccated coconut flakes.
- **UsingFrozen shredded coconut:** If you are using frozen shredded coconut, then thaw at room temperature, or soak frozen coconut in hot water for 5-10 minutes or microwave it for a few seconds before grinding. This will get you the right chutney consistency.
- **Consistency:** You can make the coconut chutney thick or thin by adjusting the water as per your preference.
- **Adjust the spiciness**: You can increase or decrease the amount of green chili according to your taste

Variations & Substitutions

- **Don't have Roasted chana dal:** Dalia or roasted chana dal thickens the chutney, so if you don't have it, then replace it with roasted peanuts, cashews, or almonds.
- **NoTamarind:** If you don't have tamarind, replace it with 1 teaspoon of lemon juice or curd. For authentic south Indian chutney recipes, tamarind is used.
- **No Ginger:** You can substitute ginger with 1-2 cloves of garlic. Ginger can be skipped completely.
- **Fresh Herbs:** You can also add fresh mint leaves and/or coriander leaves for a refreshing twist.
- **Red chilies:** To make red coconut chutney, substitute green chilies with dried red chilies.
- **Additional Flavor:** You may also add a few small shallots and curry leaves while grinding.

Onion Tomato Chutney

Ingredients

- **Onions** - I like to use red onions as they are sweeter in taste. You can also use shallots or pearl onions (sambar onions) for this recipe.

- **Tomatoes** - use fresh, ripened, and juicy tomatoes for the best taste, flavor, and color. Roma tomatoes or Red Vine Tomatoes work best. **The general rule of thumb is - the quantity of tomatoes should be twice the amount of onions in this recipe.**
- **Red Chillies** - Use Byadgi red chilies or Kashmiri Red Chillies to get a bright red color and heat to the chutney. If you don't have it, use Kashmiri red chili powder instead.
- **Garlic** - use fresh garlic cloves for the best flavor.
- **Lentils** - Roasted Urad dal adds great texture to the chutney. So don't skip it. If you don't have it, substitute it with chana dal (bengal gram).
- **Tamarind** - Adds extra tang to the chutney. You can also use store-bought tamarind paste if that is what you have in hand. If the tomatoes are too tangy, then feel free to skip this one.
- **Tempering** - mustard seeds, urad dal, curry leaves, red chili, and oil are used for tempering.

How to Make Indian Tomato Onion Chutney

Heat a tablespoon of oil in a pan on medium heat. Add split urad dal, red chilies, and saute till the dal turns light brown.

Then add garlic, curry leaves, and onion. Saute till onions turn soft and translucent.

Then add in the tomatoes, turmeric, and salt. Cook the tomatoes until they are soft and mushy, around 5-6 minutes.

Turn off the heat, add tamarind and jaggery. Mix everything well. Cool the mixture.

Once the onion tomato mixture cools, add it to mixi grinder or small blender. Grind it to a smooth paste without adding any water.

For Tempering

Heat oil in a small tadka pan, add mustard seeds, urad dal, dry red chili, and saute till the dal turns light brown.

Then add curry leaves and asafoetida (hing). Saute for a few seconds and pour the tempering over the tomato chutney.

Peanut Chutney

Ingredients

You will require very few simple ingredients to make this easy Indian peanut onion chutney recipe.

- **Peanuts - This is** the main ingredient for making this chutney. I like to use raw, unsalted peanuts for this chutney with the skin on. If you don't like the peanut skin, just rub them off when they are dry-roasted. You can also use store-bought unsalted roasted peanuts.
- **Onions** - I like to use red onions as they are sweeter in taste. You can also use shallots or pearl onions (sambar onions) for this recipe.
- **Garlic** - use fresh garlic for the best flavor.

- **Dried red chilies** - Use dried red chilies to add heat to the chutney. If you don't have it, use green chilies or red chili powder instead.
- **Split Urad Dal** - Adds great texture to the chutney, so don't skip it. If you don't have it, you can substitute it with split chana dal or white sesame seeds.
- **Cumin Seeds** - add great flavor to the chutney.
- **Tamarind** - Adds tanginess to the groundnut chutney. You can also use store-bought tamarind paste if that is what you have in hand. You may also substitute it with lemon juice or yogurt.
- **Tempering** - mustard seeds, urad dal, curry leaves, red chilies, and oil are used for this tempering.

How to Make Peanut Chutney

- Dry roast peanuts in a pan on medium flame until golden brown. Remove and let it cool down.
- In the same pan, heat oil, add cumin (jeera) seeds, split urad dal, and saute until the dal turns light brown.
- Add onion/shallots, garlic, dried red chilies and saute until the onions turn soft and light brown. It roughly takes 2-3 minutes. Turn off the heat and cool completely.
- In a blender jar, add roasted peanuts, sautéed onion-garlic mixture, tamarind, salt, water, and blend to a coarse or smooth paste as per your preference
- Heat coconut oil in a small pan, add mustard seeds, urad dal, dry red chili, curry leaves, and hing, and saute for a few seconds until the dal turns light brown
- Transfer to a bowl, and add the prepared tempering

Tips to Make the Best Peanut Chutney

- **Peanuts:** Always use good quality peanuts. Make sure that peanuts are fresh and have not gone rancid. Ensure peanuts are roasted well until golden brown on medium-low flame otherwise, they will taste raw in the chutney.
- **Lentils:** Lentils, like roasted split urad dal, adds a nutty aroma and texture to the chutney.
- **Consistency:** You can make the peanut chutney thick or thin by adjusting the water as per your preference.
- **Roasting Garlic:** Raw garlic is added in many traditional recipes, but roasting helps remove the pungent smell.
- **Tang:** Adding **tamarind** gives a tang to the chutney.

Variations

- **NoTamarind:** If you dont have tamarind, replace it with little lime juice, yogurt (curd), or amchur powder.
- **Peanuts:** You can make this chutney with or without peanut skin. Also, if you have store-bought roasted peanuts, use them directly in this recipe.

- **NoOnions:** If you dont want to use onions, replace them with the same quantity of **fresh shredded coconut**.
- **No Garlic:** You can skip the garlic and use ½ inch of ginger instead or skip both or replace it with a pinch of hing (asafetida).
- **Vegetables:** Another variation of using peanuts in chutney with roasted vegetables and chillis

Green Tomato Chutney

Ingredients

- **RawGreen Tomatoes:** Make sure you use fresh, firm raw green tomatoes. You can also use tomatillos, but the taste and texture will slightly differ.
- **Raw peanuts:** Adds great texture to the chutney, so don't skip it. You may also replace it with roasted sesame seeds, urad dal, or chana dal for a nutty flavor. You can also use store-bought roasted peanuts.
- **Garlic:** use fresh garlic for the best flavor.
- **Green chilies:** I used 4-5 Thai green chili for spicy tomato chutney. You can reduce the quantity according to your preference. You can also substitute with jalapeños.
- **Herbs:** use fresh herbs like coriander leaves, curry leaves for the best flavor.
- **Tempering** (optional) - mustard seeds, curry leaves, asafoetida, and oil are used for this tempering

How to Make Green Tomato Chutney

- In a heavy-bottomed pan, dry roast the raw peanuts until well roasted, and then keep them aside.
- In the same pan, heat one teaspoon of oil and add the green chilies. Roast them for 30 seconds or until you see blisters on their skin (you can also slit the chilies, so they don't pop)
- Then add coriander leaves, curry leaves, and saute for a minute until the leaves wilt. Keep aside
- Add another teaspoon of oil to the same pan, add sliced raw green tomato and cook until the tomatoes are charred and soft
- In a small blender, take roasted green chilies, coriander & curry leaves mixture, garlic cloves, jaggery, roasted peanuts, and salt. Blend into a coarse paste without adding water
- Then add roasted tomatoes and blend to a coarse or smooth chutney without adding any water

Variations

- **Nutty-Flavor:** Do not skip adding peanuts they give body to the chutney and enhance the taste. Don't add more you will end up with peanut chutney. If you want to make it nut-free, you can substitute it with roasted sesame seeds, chana dal, or urad dal.

- **Spicy:** Increase or decrease the green chilies according to your spice level.
- **Tangy:** I have not added tamarind to this recipe since the green tomatoes I used were tart. If you want, you can add a small piece of tamarind.
- **SkipGarlic:** If you don't like garlic, or for a no-garlic recipe, skip it and replace it with ¼ teaspoon of hing (asafoetida).
- **Tempering:** You can also add tempering (tadka) to the chutney, but it's totally optional

Ragi idli

INGREDIENTS

- Ragi flour - 2 cups
- Idli rice - 1 cup
- Urad dal - 1/2 cup
- Methi seeds -2 tsp
- Salt & water - as needed

HOW TO MAKE RAGI IDLI - METHOD

- Wash and soak the rice,dal & methi seeds together for two hours. Add the required water and grind everything all together adding required salt & water. Lastly add the ragi flour, grind for few minutes.Remove and ferment overnight or 10 hours.
- The next day, batter would be doubled and sometimes overflown too. Stir well and make idlies.
- Steam in idli mould for 10-12 minutes till the inserted spoon comes out clean.
- U can make dosas by diluting the batter slightly. Make crispy or soft dosas as per ur need.
- Enjoy with chutney

For variations, you can use whole ragi grains instead of flour.

- If you want to try without rice, use 3: 1 ratio of ragi flour and urad dal. Add 2 tbsp of poha for softness.
- While making idli, you can add tempered and saute onions, green chillies, ginger & curry leaves as it makes the idli flavorful.

Kushboo Idli

INGREDIENTS

- 1 cup = 250ml or 200ml (use same cup to measure all ingredients)
- Idli rice / Salem rice / parboiled rice – 2 cups
- Urad dal – 1/2 cup
- Sago / Javvarisi / sabudana – 1/4 cup (White big ones, not the crystal nylon variety)
- Salt and water – As needed. (Use ice water if using mixie to grind batter)

HOW TO MAKE KUSHBOO IDLI

- Wash and soak idli rice, sago and urad dal separately in sufficient water.
- Soak for minimum 4 hours. First grind the urad dal to a smooth, thick paste adding little ice water in a mixie or grinder.
- Collect the batter in a bowl. Grind rice + sago together adding required ice water.
- Mix rice batter and urad dal batter with your hand. Ferment over night or 15 hours.
- The next morning, batter would have raised. Add salt and mix well.
- Spread wet cotton cloth over idli plate. Pour the batter in each hole.
- Roll boil water in an idli pot. Place the idli plate and steam for 10 minutes.
- Remove the idli plate and invert it over another plate. Sprinkle water all over the cloth.
- Now you can easily remove the cloth. Hot, fluffy, spongy, white Kushboo idli is ready !

METHOD - STEP BY STEP

- Wash the idli rice thrice and soak in enough water. Washing the rice properly helps to give white colored idli. Wash the urad dal once and soak it. Wash the sago once and soak it. Soak everything separately for minimum 4 hours.
- Take a big sized mixie jar. You can grind in grinder too. Firstly grind the soaked urad dal to a smooth paste adding little ice water. Collect the batter in a big bowl. Next grind the soaked rice and sago together in 2 batches. Grind to a smooth batter adding sufficient ice water. Do not use more water
- Mix urad dal batter and rice, sago batter using your hand. Cover and allow the batter to ferment overnight or minimum 15 hours based on the weather in your place
- The next morning, batter would have raised well. Add required salt and mix well. Consistency of batter should be like our regular idli dosa batter. It should be thick and pourable.
- Now take an idli plate and spread a wet cloth over it. Pour ladleful of batter in each hole. Roll boil water in an idli pot. Place the idli plate over it. Cover and steam the idli for 10 minutes. Dip your forefinger in water and make a hole in one of the idli. If your finger comes out clean, idli is cooked. If your finger is sticky, cook for few more minutes. Switch off the flame and rest the idli inside the pot for few minutes.

- To remove the idli, take the idli plate and invert it over another empty plate. Sprinkle water over the wet cloth and remove the cloth gently. Idli comes out smooth and super soft.

Idli Rava

INGREDIENTS

- 1 cup - 250ml
- Idli rava – 2 cups
- White round urad dal – 1/2 cup (If you follow the video recipe, please use 1/3 cup)
- Water – 1-1.25 cups (Use Ice cold water)
- Salt – As needed

METHOD

- Wash and soak the Idli rava and urad dal together in a bowl for 45 minutes. Drain the soaked water completely before grinding. (In the video I have mentioned to soak them & grind separately. Add 1/3 cup of urad dal in that case. This method needs less urad dal.)
- Grind half of its amount in mixie adding 1/2 cup of ice cold water & the required salt for 3-5 minutes.After 2 mins , open the lid , wipe the sides & grind again. Add little more water if its necessary.
- Again grind the remaining mixture adding 1/2 cup of water. (Note : Batter will be slightly coarse even if you grind for long time , no need to worry) Mix both the batter using your hand. (Mixing by hand helps for fermentation). Keep the bowl closed & allow the batter to ferment for 8- 15 hrs based on the weather in your place.
- The next morning, batter would have raised well . Mix it well before making idlies. Pour the batter in idli plate , steam it for 6-8 mins & enjoy with ur favourite chutney !!

Note

- The maximum amount of water it consumes while grinding is 1.25 –1.5 cups. Adjust as per your mixer. I used ice cold water to avoid the mixer getting heated. Plain water can also be used.
- Fermentation is very important to get soft, non-sticky idlies.
- People suggest idli rava & dal ratio as 3:1. But 4:1 is enough for soft idlies.
- If you want, you can add a tsp of soaked fenugreek seeds too to make it healthy.
- U can also make crispy dosa using the same batter

Brown Rice Idli

INGREDIENTS

- 1 cup = 250ml
- Brown rice - 2.5 cups
- Urad dal - 1/2 cup
- Aval/poha-1/4 cup
- Methi seeds - 1/2 tsp
- Salt & water - as needed

HOW TO MAKE BROWN RICE IDLI - METHOD

- Wash the brown rice 2-3 times. Soak rice, urad dal,methi seeds,poha together for 5 hours.
- Now drain the water and grind them in the grinder adding salt & water. Add water in regular intervals. This takes nearly 20-25 minutes for grinding. It too 2.5 – 3 cups of water ..Remove the batter and allow it to ferment for 8 hours or overnight.
- The next day, batter would have raised well. Mix the batter and make idlis.. It takes around 15-18 mins to cook. Check with the spoon or wet your finger and make a hole in the center of the idli , if your finger comes out clean, idli is cooked..Serve hot with chutney

Oats Idli

INGREDIENTS

- 1 cup = 200ml
- To roast and grind
- Quaker Oats - 1 cup
- To make batter
- Wheat rava - 1/2 cup
- Curd - 1/2 cup
- Grated carrots - 3 tbsp
- Grated cabbage – 1.5 tbsp
- Green peas - 2 tbsp
- Salt - as needed
- Water - 3/4 - 1 cup (adjust)
- Ginger - 1 inch piece
- Green chillies - 1-2 nos (finely chopped)

- Pepper corns - 1/2 tsp
- Lemon juice - few drops
- Eno fruit salt –3/4 tsp
- Coriander leaves - 2 tbsp (finely chopped)
- To temper
- Cooking oil - 2 tsp
- Mustard seeds - 1/2 tsp
- Urad dal - 1 tsp
- Chana dal - 1 tsp
- Curry leaves - few
- Hing - a pinch

METHOD

- Dry roast oats in a kadai for 2-3 minutes in medium flame.Powder it nicely.
- In a kadai,heat oil and temper all the ingredients given above in the same order.Add the grated carrots,cabbage and peas.Saute for a minute.Now add the wheat rava & powdered oats flour.Roast for 2 minutes.Add salt and remove.Let it cool for 10 minutes.
- Then add curd,water and make a thick batter like idli batter.
- Add Eno fruit salt,coriander leaves and lemon juice.Mix well.Grease the idli plate and pour the batter.
- Steam in a idli pot for 15 minutes.Check for doneness by inserting a knife or spoon.
- Remove and enjoy

Kanchipuram Idli

INGREDIENTS

- Par Boiled rice / idli rice – 1/2 cup
- Raw rice – 1/2 cup
- Urad dal – 1/2 cup
- Pepper corns – 1/2 tsp
- Jeera – 1/2 tsp
- Ghee – 2 tbsp
- Sesame / Gingely oil – 2 tbsp
- Hing / Asafetida – 1/2 tsp
- Curry leaves – a few

- Dry ginger / Sukku – 1/2 inch piece (crushed) (optional) (you can use powder too)
- Salt – as required.

HOW TO MAKE KANCHIPURAM IDLI - METHOD

- Soak the dal and rice together for 2-3 hours. Wash , drain the water and grind .
- Please don't add more water to grind.The batter should be thick and little coarse.
- After grinding the batter add salt , hing and mix well. Allow the batter to ferment overnight. The next day morning add crushed pepper , jeera , dry ginger powder , curry leaves , Ghee and sesame oil to the batter and mix well.
- If u feel the batter is too thick, add a ladleful of water to it. Do not disturb the batter for 30 mins- 1 hour. After 1 hour , place the banana leaf on the idly plate and pour the batter.
- Steam it for 15 to 30 mins.Once its done ,prick the idly with the backside of spoon and see whether the idlI is non sticky . At this stage the idli is cooked well.
- Remove and serve hot with coconut chutney

Oats Barley Idli

INGREDIENTS

- 1 cup - 200ml
- Barley - 1 cup
- Idli rice – 1 cup
- Urad dal - 1/4 cup
- Quick oats - 1/2 cup
- Salt & water – as needed

METHOD

- Wash and soak all the above ingredients for 5 hours. Before soaking , rinse and drain for 2-3 times to remove the dust in barley. Grind it smooth by adding the required water and salt.
- Ferment it for a minimum of 12 hrs or over night.
- The next day,batter would have raised or sometimes doubled. (based on weather)
- Make idlies by steaming in idli pot.It takes about 15-20 mins for cooking. Check it by inserting the tip of the spoon. If it comes out clean,idli is cooked.
- U can make crispy dosas also by adding water to the batter. Dilute the batter,mix well and make dosas.

Foxtail Millet Idli

INGREDIENTS

- 1 cup = 250ml
- Foxtail millet/Thinai - 2.5 cups
- Idli rice/Salem rice - 1/2 cup
- Urad dal - 1/2 cup
- Aval/Poha - 1/4 cup
- Fenugreek seeds - 1/2 tsp
- Salt & water - as needed

HOW TO MAKE THINAI IDLI - METHOD

- Measure & take all the ingredients together and wash it carefully . Its better if you wash it using a strainer. Soak for 3-4 hours.
- Grind them to a smooth paste adding required water and salt. Remove mix well and allow it to ferment overnight or minimum 8 hours.
- The next day, batter would have raised well(Not doubled). Now mix the batter very well and pour in a idli plate.
- Boil water in a idli pan and keep the plates. Steam it for 10-15 minutes. Check with the back of a spoon for doneness. If the spoon comes out clean, idli is ready.
- Remove the idli plate and rest it for 2-3 minutes before removing them else it will be sticky.
- Refrigerate the batter & make dosas the next day.

Thatte Idli

INGREDIENTS

- 1 cup - 250ml
- Idli rice/Salem rice - 2 cups
- Raw rice - 1 cup (use dosa rice)
- Urad dal - 3/4 cup (white round or split urad dal)
- Thick poha OR Cooked rice - 1/2 cup
- Salt & water - as needed
- Cooking soda / Baking soda - 1/4 tsp

HOW TO MAKE THATTE IDLI -METHOD

- Wash and soak all the ingredients together for 4 hours. Do not drain the water after it is soaked. Grind it well to a smooth paste using the water you used for soaking. Add more water if necessary.(U can use cooked rice while grinding too. No need to soak it. If using poha, soak it with rice.)
- It takes nearly 30 minutes to grind in a grinder. Add salt if summer season, mix the batter well and allow it to ferment overnight. U should leave it for at least 12 hours. Proper fermentation is needed to get soft idlis.
- Next morning, add salt and cooking soda. Mix well and rest for 15 minutes before you make idlis. Mix well.
- Add water in a cooker base & allow it to boil. Take the thatte idli stand and grease all plates with oil generously. You can use some white cotton cloth or banana leaf too. Pour the batter and keep the stand in cooker. Cook for 12-15 minutes. (Stepwise pictures Updated)
- If you don't have thatte idli stand, take a small round plate with rim.I used the lid of steel storage containers. Grease with oil generously or line with the cloth & pour the batter.
- Take the idli pot with water & boil. Keep the round plate over the idli plate and cook for 10-15 minutes. Check with the back of spoon. If it comes out clean,idli is cooked. Allow the idlis to cool for few seconds before u remove them else it may break. If you have thatte idli stand, keep it inside the idli steamer and cook for 10 minutes.

Bajra Idli

INGREDIENTS

- Pearl millet / Bajra - 2 cups
- White,round urad dal - 1/2 cup
- Poha / Aval / rice flakes - 1/4 cup (I used thick poha)
- Methi seeds / Fenugreek seeds - 1/2 tsp (Optional)
- Salt & Water - As needed

HOW TO MAKE PEARL MILLET IDLI

- Wash and soak pearl millet, methi seeds and poha together for 5 hours.
- Wash and soak urad dal separately in another bowl for 2 hours.
- Grind urad dal to a smooth paste adding the soaked water.
- Collect in a bowl and then grind millet + Poha mixture to a smooth paste adding enough water.
- Mix both the batter with hands and let it ferment overnight. The next day, mix the batter well and make idli.

Mini Masala Idli Tadka:

- Cut each idli into quarter pieces or small cubes or any size of your choice.

- Heat the pan by adding cooking oil.
- Let the mustard seeds splutter.
- Add urad dal and wait for few a seconds.
- Add curry leaves and give it a toss.
- Add roughly chopped mini idlis. Let it fry on a medium flame for some minutes.
- Finally, chop cilantro leaves and add it into the mini idli pan.
- Toss for some more time, say 2-3 minutes.
- Finally, serve your dish.

Your mini masala idli tadka is ready. You can enjoy this dish with any chutney of your choice. You can have idli masala with coconut chutney, tomato chutney, or green chutney. If you are a coconut lover, you can also add small coconut chunks into this idli masala. Idli masala is also a highly customizable dish. You can add any masala of your choice

Schezwan idli

Ingredients

- 4 idlis
- 2 tbsp spring onion whites
- 2 -3 tsp schezwan sauce
- 2 tbsp oil
- 2 tbsp capsicum
- 1 tbsp spring onion greens

Instructions

- Cut the idlis into 4 pieces.
- In a pan add 1 tbsp oil and saute the idlis for 3-4 minutes. This step is optional. You can skip this too.
- Once all the idlis are coated well in oil and turns slightly brown take it out and keep aside.
- In the same pan add 1 tbsp oil and add spring onion whites. If you don't have spring onion, you can use finely chopped onions too.
- Saute the spring onion whites for 1-2 minutes.
- Add the capsicum to this and saute this for a minute.
- I used red and yellow capsicum.
- Add 2 tsp of schezwan sauce. If you want a lttle spicier, you can add 1 tsp extra too.
- Mix well and add the idlis now.

- Gently mix and evenly coat all the idlis in the sacue.
- Cook for a minute in high flame.
- Switch off and garnish with spring onion greens.
- Schezwan Idli is ready to serve.

NOTE: You can replace sauce make tomato base , pesto base sauce

CHAPTER TEN

Pancakes

Pancake recipe

INGREDIENTS

- 2 cup maida / plain flour / refined flour
- 2 tbsp sugar
- 1 tbsp baking powder
- ½ tsp baking soda
- pinch of salt
- 2 tbsp butter (melted)
- 1½ cup milk
- butter for serving
- honey for serving

INSTRUCTIONS

- firstly, in a large mixing bowl take 2 cups maida. you can alternatively use wheat flour / atta for a healthy option.
- also add 2 tbsp sugar, 1 tbsp baking powder, ½ tsp baking soda and a pinch of salt.
- mix well combining all the dry ingredients well.
- further add 2 tbsp melted butter, 1 cup milk and combine well with the whisk.
- additionally, add ½ cup more milk and make smooth flowing consistency batter.
- heat a nonstick pan and grease with butter. pour a ladleful of prepared pancake batter. do not spread.
- simmer and cook for 2 minutes or until bubbles appear on the surface.
- flip over the pancakes and simmer for 1-2 minutes or until cooked through.
- finally, serve eggless pancake with some butter and honey or maple syrup on top.

NOTES:

- firstly, to make pancake softer, use buttermilk in place of milk.
- also, add banana puree to make eggless banana pancake recipe.
- additionally, use non-stick pan to make pancakes, else it will be difficult to flip over.
- finally, **eggless pancake** tastes great when served warm so cover with a foil once prepared.

Potato Pancake

This pancake can be made using leftover mashed potatoes or hash browns and it is a perfect breakfast pancake recipe for toddlers.

Ingredients

- 1 ½ cup mashed potatoes
- 1 cup Maida
- 1 cup milk
- I tbsp chopped chives
- 1 tsp baking powder
- 1 tsp any vegetable oil
- A dollop of butter

How to make

1. Take a big glass bowl put mashed potatoes into it.
2. Sieve baking powder and flour over the mashed potatoes.
3. Add milk and maida to the bowl and mix all the ingredients well or till the batter is smooth.
4. Put chopped chives into and batter and mix well.
5. Heat the pan over medium heat and grease it with oil and a hint of butter.
6. Pour the pancake mix and cook on both sides until it turns golden brown.

Almond Flour Pancake

This healthy pancake recipe can be used as a yummy picnic treat.

Ingredients

- 1 cup almond flour
- 1 Cup Butter Milk
- 1 tsp coconut oil
- ¼ tsp salt

- ¼ cup water
- 1 tbsp maple syrup

How to make

1. Mix almond flour, buttermilk, water, maple syrup and salt in a big mixing bowl. Whisk until the batter turns smooth and lump free.
2. Turn on the gas stove and heat the pan over medium heat.
3. Grease the pan with coconut oil.
4. Drop the batter on the pan and cook the pancakes from both the sides till they turn golden brown.
5. Pour some maple syrup on top before serving.

Cinnamon And Oatmeal Pancakes

This aromatic pancake recipe will be a hit with your little one.
Ingredients

- 1 ½ cup oatmeal
- ½ cup milk
- ½ cup butter milk
- ½ tsp cinnamon powder
- ¼ tsp nutmeg powder
- ½ tbsp sugar
- ¼ tsp baking powder
- A pinch of salt

How to make

1. Take a large bowl and mix all the ingredients together in it.
2. Make sure the batter does not get too thin or runny; you may add extra oatmeal to work upon the consistency of the batter.
3. Heat any non-stick pan on medium flame.
4. Grease the pan and gradually pour pancake mix.
5. Cook the pancakes well from both the sides.
6. You may serve the pancakes with any topping or with any syrup of your choice.

There are lots of ways to top pancakes. Here are a few your kids might like.

- Peanut butter, almond butter, chocolate hazelnut spread, chopped nuts
- Maple syrup or honey
- Fresh jam or preserves
- Fresh fruits such as sliced bananas or berries of any kind
- Whipped cream and chocolate sauce takes it more toward dessert
- You can use ready to use pancake mix or dosa better can be replaced

CHAPTER ELEVEN

Rice Preparations

Raw Mango Rice

Ingredients needed

- Cooked Rice – 3 cup
- Grated mango -1 cup
- Turmeric powder – 1/4 tsp
- Salt as needed

For the seasoning

- Oil – 2 tsp
- Mustard seeds -1 tsp
- Bengal gram/channa dal -2 tsp
- Urad dal -1 1/2 tsp
- Red chillies -2 (break it into 2 pieces)
- Hing -a pinch
- Green chillies -2 slit
- Peanuts -1/4 cup
- Curry leaves – few

Preparation

- Cook rice in such a way that each grain remains separate. Spread it on a plate to cool.
- Wash, peel and grate raw mangoes.

- Fry peanuts separately and keep it aside. (You can also fry along with dal in medium flame but should take care not to burn the peanuts)

Method

- Heat oil in a pan, add mustard seeds, when it splutters, add bengal gram, urad dal, red chillies, green chillies and hing.
- When dal turns golden brown, add peanuts, turmeric powder, salt needed and curry leaves.
- Add grated mangoes and mix well to combine with the spices. Cook for just 2-3 seconds and switch off the flame.
- Add cooked rice and mix gently using a fork taking care not to break the rice. Check for salt, add if required.
- Enjoy mango rice with chips or papads as side dish.

Notes – Use sour/tangy mangoes for this dish. If your mangoes are not sour enough, then add a little more than 1 cup.

You can add cashew nuts instead of peanuts if you prefer.

Lemon Rice

Ingredients:

- 1 cup cooked rice (warm or hot temp.)
- half a lemon
- 1 tsp mustard seeds
- 1tsp *urad* dal
- 2 dry chillies
- one long sliced green chilli
- 8-9 curry leaves
- ¼ peanuts (dry fried or sautéed)
- ½ tsp turmeric
- salt

Preparation:

- Temper mustard seeds and sauté *urad* dal. Add the chillies (dry and green) and curry leaves.
- Once they change colour, switch off the flame.
- Mix hing, turmeric and salt to the tempering.
- Spread the rice evenly in a pan. Add the above mixture and then squeeze the lemon. Mix well.

- Add coriander to garnish.

Rice Cutlets

Ingredients:

- 1 cup of cooked rice
- ½ cup boiled potato
- I chopped onion
- 1 chopped green chilly
- ¼ cup chopped coriander
- ¼ tsp of red chilli, turmeric and coriander powder each
- ½ tsp *chat masala*
- 3 tbsp. gram flour
- salt
- oil

Preparation:

- Mix and mash all ingredients one after the other in a bowl (except oil). Add or reduce the spices or salt according to your taste.
- Make small or medium-sized patties and shallow fry in a pan. They are well done when they are golden brown.

Carrot rice

Ingredients

- 2 cups cooked rice
- 1.5 cups Carrot grated
- 2 tablespoon Moong dal refer notes for options
- 1 Onion
- 2 Green chilli slit
- ⅛ teaspoon Turmeric
- 1 teaspoon Sambar powder
- 2 teaspoon Ghee
- Salt

Instructions

1. Prep all the ingredients required.
2. First wash rice, dal and soak it in hot water for 15 - 30 mins.
3. Cook rice with water ratio 1 : 1 & ½ cups for 3 whistles. Once done, spread in a plate and cool down.
4. After that, clean, peel and grate carrot. I used a julienne grater and then chopped it by stacking roughly.
5. Heat a pan with oil, temper with mustard, urad dal, curry leaves, green chillies.
6. In goes soaked & drained moong dal. Give it a roast in low flame for a minute.
7. Then add finely chopped onion and saute until it is soft.
8. Following that, add the grated carrot. Add required salt, turmeric, sambar powder and give a a roast.
9. Splash about 2 to 3 tablespoon of water and give it a mix.
10. Cook covered for 2 minutes in low flame.
11. Once done, give it a mix. If too dry you can add a drizzle of oil. Add cooked rice and grated coconut.
12. Mix carefully to heat it up and rice becomes uniformly colored.
13. Finally add ghee and switch off the stove.
14. Hint: If you are adding cashews you can ghee fry it and add it now.

SUBSTITUTIONS

- **Onion** - If you want to make this a no onion no garlic carrot rice, feel free to skip it. If you like you can add little asafoetida for flavor.
- **Rice** - any leftover rice form your previous meal can be used. Be it parboiled or raw rice like sona masoori, you can just follow the same recipe. Millets can also be replace for rice.
- **Coconut** - Coconut can also be skipped, you can try coconut oil for giving similar flavor.
- **Moong dal** - You can skip moong dal and add peanuts too for added protein.

MASALA RICE

Ingredients

- Rice - 1 cup
- Big Onion - 1 medium sized
- Tomato - 1 medium sized
- Green chilli - 1
- Ginger- 1 teaspoon chopped
- Turmeric powder - ¼ tsp

- Sambar powder/ Pav Bhaji Masala - 1 tbsp
- Chopped Vegetables* -1 cup
- Coriander leaves - a handful
- Water - 1.5 cups
- Salt - as required
- To temper
- Ghee/Oil - 2 tbsp
- Mustard seeds - ½ tsp
- cumin seeds - ½ tsp
- Urad Dal - ¼ tsp
- Hing - a generous pinch
- I have used carrots beans, chopped cauliflower and green capsicum

Instructions

- Wash rice and soak it in water for 20 minutes. Wash and chop all vegetables into cubes. Slice onions, chop ginger and tomatoes finely. Slit green chilies. Roughly chop coriander leaves. Set aside.
- Heat a pressure cooker with ghee or oil. Add mustard seeds,cumin seeds,hing and urad dal. Let mustard seeds crackle. Then add onions along with ginger & green chillies. Saute them nicely until golden brown.
- Once onions becomes transparent , add tomatoes along with salt, turmeric powder and sambar powder/phav bhaji masala powder. Fry tomatoes until the raw smell of tomatoes leaves and become mushy.
- Now add chopped vegetables and toss them nicely for 3 minutes. Then add soaked rice.
- Mix well. Add water (1.5 cups of water) and bring it to a boil.Add in coriander leaves at this stage. Then close the lid of pressure cooker and cook everything in a medium flame for three to four whistles.
- Once the pressure releases, open the cooker and fluff the rice with a spoon slowly, top with ghee if required. Garnish with coriander leaves.

TAVA PULAO

Ingredients

- 1 cup Basmati rice or long grain rice
- 1 medium sized potato peeled and chopped
- 1 medium sized onion finely chopped
- 2 medium sized tomatoes finely chopped
- 1/2 capsicum chopped

- 1 small carrot peeled and chopped
- 1/4 cup green peas
- 1 tablespoon ginger-garlic paste made from ½ inch ginger and 4 to 5 garlic pods
- 1 Green Chili finely chopped
- 2 tablespoon pav bhaji masala
- 1 teaspoon red chili powder
- 1 teaspoon cumin powder
- 1/4 teaspoon turmeric powder
- 1 bay leaf
- 1 tablespoon lemon juice
- 2 tablespoon Butter
- 1 teaspoon oil
- Few Coriander Leaves finely chopped for garnish
- To taste Salt

Instructions

1. Wash basmati rice or long grain rice and keep it aside for 30 minutes.
2. Cook the basmati rice in a pot to which 4 to 5 cups water, 1/4 teaspoon salt and bay leaf is added. The rice should be par-boiled and should not be sticky.
3. Drain the rice on a colander and let it cool down. Fluff it with a fork.
4. Boil vegetables like potato, carrot and green peas. Drain the water and keep the boiled vegetables aside.
5. Heat a tava or large frying pan. Add 1 tablespoon butter and 1 teaspoon oil.
6. Add finely chopped onion and sauté till onions turn pinkish.
7. Add ginger garlic paste and sauté till aroma of garlic goes away.
8. Add finely chopped tomato and sauté till tomatoes turn mushy.
9. Add chopped capsicum (bell pepper) and sauté till capsicum is cooked.
10. Add the spice powders (masala) like pav bhaji masala, red chili powder, turmeric powder and cumin powder and mix well. Cook for 5 minutes.
11. Add the boiled vegetables like potato, green peas and carrot and mix well.
12. Using a potato masher, mash all the vegetables just like how we do while doing pav bhaji. If needed add ¼ cup water.
13. Add salt and mix well.
14. Next add the cooked rice to the tava and mix gently.
15. Taste and add more salt if needed and mix.

16. Garnish with chopped coriander leaves, lemon juice and a blob of butter.

SOYA PULAO

Ingredients

- 1 Cup Basmati rice
- 1 medium sized onion finely chopped
- 4 Garlic Pods finely chopped
- 1/2 carrot julienned
- 1/4 red bell pepper julienned
- 5 tablespoon soya granules
- 1 tablespoon lemon juice
- 2 tablesoon oil
- To taste Salt

Grind the following:

- 20 pudina/mint leaves
- 2 tablespoon corriander leaves chopped
- 3 pods garlic peeled
- 1 Green Chili
- 1/4 inch ginger peeled

Spices:

- 1 bay leaf
- 5 black pepper corns
- 2 cloves
- 1 inch cinnamon
- 3 cardamom pods crushed
- 1/2 teaspoon cumin seeds / jeera

Instructions

1. Wash the soya granules and soak for 15 minutes. Wash the rice and keep aside for 15 minutes. Grind the ingredients mentioned in grind section by adding 2 tablespoon water.
2. Drain the water from soya granules and squeeze out excess water.
3. Pour the ground paste on soya granules and let it get marinated for 10 minutes.
4. Heat cooker and add oil to it. Add all the spices and let oil get infused with the spices.
5. Then add finely chopped onion and sauté till it becomes pinkish. Add garlic and stir.
6. Add carrots and bell pepper and stir.
7. After 5 minutes, add washed rice and stir for 3-4 minutes.
8. Next add the marinated soya granules along with pudina paste. Add salt to taste. Add lemon juice and mix.
9. Add a little less than 2 cups water and pressure cook for 2 whistles on low flame. After 2 whistles, switch of the gas and let the pulao get cooked internally.
10. After 15 minutes, loosen the lid and wait for the pressure to be released.

MEXICAN RICE

Ingredients

- 1 and ½ cups Basmati rice
- 1 small carrot diced
- 1 small red bell pepper diced
- 1 medium sized onion finely chopped
- 4 garlic pods minced
- ½ cup tomato puree
- 1 jalapeno or green chili finely chopped
- 1 teaspoon black pepper powder
- ½ teaspoon cumin powder
- 1 teaspoon red chili powder or paprika
- 2 tablespoon oil
- 3 cups vegetable stock or water
- To taste salt

Instructions

1. Wash Basmati rice under running tap water 2-3 times, drain and keep it aside for minimum 30 minutes.
2. Heat a pan and add oil. After oil gets heated add onion and sauté till onion turns pinkish.
3. Add garlic and fry till garlic turns aromatic.

4. Add washed rice and stir well till the rice starts getting brownish.
5. Add vegetables like chopped carrots, chopped bell pepper, green peas, green chili or jalapeño and sweet corn.
6. Add seasonings like black pepper powder, cumin powder, paprika or red chili powder, tomato puree or sauce and salt to taste and mix well.
7. Add vegetable stock or water and mix well. If needed add little more salt after tasting the broth.
8. Cover the pan with a lid and cook covered for 20 minutes on low flame till the rice is cooked and all water is absorbed.
9. Switch off the heat and let the rice sit covered for 5 minutes.
10. After 5 minutes, using a fork or spoon fluff the rice gently.
11. Garnish with finely chopped coriander.

BEETROOT PULAO

Ingredients:

- 1 1/2 cup Basmati Rice
- 2 bay leaves
- 2-3 peppercorns
- 2-3 cloves
- 1 teaspoon mustard seeds
- 1 teaspoon cumin seeds
- 1 teaspoon urad dal / black gram dal
- 5-6 curry leaves
- 2 red chilies
- 1 teaspoon cumin powder
- 1 teaspoon coriander powder
- 1 teaspoon cinnamon powder
- 1/2 teaspoon asafoetida
- 1/2 teaspoon chili powder
- 2 medium sized beetroot
- 2 medium sized onions
- 1 tomato
- 1 tablespoon ginger-garlic paste
- 2 tablespoon sunflower oil

Instructions:

- First wash the rice and keep aside for 10 minutes.
- Boil the rice with 5 cups water. to this add bay leaves, peppercorns and cloves.
- This will add better flavour to the rice. To this add 1/2 tablespoon salt.
- Let it be semi-boiled.
- Now spread the rice on a big strainer and let it cool down. For faster cooling keep the rice under the fan.
- On this add Cinnamon powder.
- Meanwhile, in a wok add oil.
- When the oil gets heated, add mustard seeds. Once they splutter add curry leaves.
- Add the black gram dal, asafoetida and red chillies.
- To this add finely chopped onions.
- When the onions fry, add ginger garlic paste
- Saute these for some time and then add finely chopped tomato.
- To this add cumin, coriander and chilly powder.
- After 5 minutes, add the grated beetroot. Fry for 10 minutes by keeping the wok covered.
- Once these gets fried add 1/4 tablespoon salt or as per taste.
- Now add the rice and mix properly, ensuring that the grains does not break.
- Garnish with chopped coriander leaves.

CAULIFLOWER RICE

Ingredients

- 1 cup Basmati rice
- 1 cup Cauliflower florets
- 2 medium sized onion cut lengthwise
- 5 Garlic Pods minced
- 1 teaspoon ginger-garlic paste
- 1 inch cinnamon stick
- 4 cloves
- 5 black peppercorns
- 1 bayleaf
- 1 teaspoon Black Pepper Powder
- 1/2 teaspoon cinnamon powder
- 2 tablespoon Coriander Leaves chopped
- 2 tablespoon oil

Instructions

1. Wash basmati rice and drain water. Keep washed basmati rice aside for 20 minutes.
2. Wash basmati rice and drain water. Keep washed basmati rice aside for 20 minutes.
3. After it's done, fluff it using a fork. Sprinkle black pepper powder and cinnamon powder on the cooked basmati rice and keep it aside. See notes on how to cook rice.
4. Meanwhile, heat a kadai/wok and add oil.
5. After oil gets heated, add the spices, namely cinnamon, cloves and black peppercorns. Sauté for half a minute.
6. Add onion and sauté till onion turns pinkish.
7. Add minced garlic and sauté.
8. Next add ginger garlic paste and sauté.
9. Add coriander leaves and mix well.
10. Next add cauliflower florets and cook it covered on low flame for 5 minutes. Ensure that the broccoli florets remain bit crunchy. Don't over-cook them.
11. Next add salt to taste and mix.
12. In the last step, add rice and toss ensuring that the long grains of basmati rice does not break.

Vegetable rice salad

Ingredients:

- Boiled rice – 1 cup
- Grated raw vegetables (tomatoes, cabbage, beet root, onions) – 1 cup
- Salt as per taste

Process:

- Add chopped vegetables, salt to boiled rice. This recipe can be given to your toddlers and kids.
- It can also be given to babies (use grated vegetables) above one year if they have teeth, are able to chew and also have no issues with digestion of raw vegetables and fruits.

CHAPTER TWELVE

Healthy Vegetable Curries

Vegetable Stir-Fry With Bengali Five-Spice and Split Peas

Ingredients

- 1 tablespoon oil (preferably mustard or olive oil)
- 11/2 teaspoons panchphoron (Bengali Five Spice Blend)
- 1-2 dried red chili peppers
- 1 red onion, chopped
- 2 small red potatoes, cubed
- 2 medium carrots, peeled and diced
- 1 cup of green beans, cut into 1/2-inch pieces
- 1/4 cup split peas, soaked overnight
- Salt, to taste
- Chopped fresh cilantro, to garnish

Preparation

1. In a large cooking pot, heat the oil and add in the panchphoron and wait until the seeds begin to crackle, andthen add in the dried red chilis.
2. In a few minutes, add in the red onion and cook for about 3-4 minutes.
3. Add in all the vegetables and the split peas with a little salt and about 1/2 cup water.
4. Cover and cook for 10 minutes. Remove the cover and cook until the water is evaporated.
5. Garnish with cilantro and serve.

Chana Saag

Ingredients

Here are some of the main ingredients you will need for this recipe:

- Chickpeas - I am using canned chickpeas in this recipe but you can use dry chickpeas instead. Please see my notes in the recipe card below for tips on using dried chickpeas.
- Greens - I love to add spinach but you can also use methi, mustard greens, or a mix.
- Tomatoes - Diced fresh tomatoes or canned tomatoes with liquids work well.
- Ginger and Garlic Paste - I prefer using homemade ginger and garlic paste but storebought ones work equally well.
- Spices - Garam Masala, Mild Kashmiri Red Chili, Turmeric is all that you will need. If you do not have dry mango powder, simply squeeze some fresh lemon in the end.

How to make Chana Masala

- In a medium-sized pot, add ghee and when it's sizzling hot, toss in the chopped onions and salt and saute for 5 to 7 minutes or until they are translucent.
- Next, add the ginger and garlic, and sauté for an additional 2 to 3 minutes as the onions continue to brown.
- Add the chopped tomato, turmeric, red chili powder, and ground cumin.

- Stir well and cook covered for 2 to 3 minutes or just until the tomatoes start to soften. Add half a cup of warm water, lower the heat to medium and let the spices infuse the tomato for another 2 to 3 minutes.
- Stir in the chickpeas and cook for another 2 to 3 minutes as the chickpeas are heated through. Add the spinach, stir into the masala, and cook just until the spinach wilts. Turn the heat off.
- Add garam masala and amchoor powder or lemon juice. Mix well

Mixed Vegetable Curry

INGREDIENTS

- 3 tablespoon cooking oil
- 1 teaspoon cumin seeds
- 1 medium red onion sliced fine
- 1 teaspoon chopped ginger
- 1 teaspoon chopped garlic
- 2 small tomatoes chopped
- 1 teaspoon coriander powder
- 1 teaspoon red chilli powder
- ½ teaspoon turmeric powder

- salt to taste
- 1 cup sweet peas
- 1 cup diced carrots
- 2 cups cauliflower florets
- 1 cup diced French beans
- 1.5 cups diced potatoes

INSTRUCTIONS

Heat the oil in a deep pan or karahi (wok) and add the cumin seeds and onions.

1. Fry the onions until they start to caramelize and turn brown.
2. Add the ginger, garlic and tomatoes. Cook until the tomatoes break down and soften. You can add a splash of water if the masala is too dry.
3. Add the spices (coriander, red chilli and turmeric) and salt and stir well.
4. Add the remaining vegetables - peas, carrots, cauliflower, beans and potatoes. Add a splash of water, mix and cover the pan. Cook on low-medium heat until the vegetables are cooked through but not mushy. Serve hot with Indian bread like roti or paratha.

NOTES

- Don't add too much water or the vegetables will turn mushy.
- Chop or dice the vegetables into small even sized pieces to allow for uniform cooking.
- You can substitute with other vegetables like bell peppers, baby corn, mushrooms or cabbage.
- For an interesting variation, add paneer or tofu depending upon your dietary preferences.
- You can use frozen vegetables too in this recipe, but remember not to add any water in this case.
- For a spicy curry, add a couple of slit green chillies and a pinch of garam masala

BHINDI SABZI

INGREDIENTS

- 300 Gram Bhindi
- ¼ cup mustard or olive oil
- 2 cups red onions sliced
- 1 teaspoon cumin seeds
- ½ teaspoon turmeric

- 2 dry red chillies
- salt to taste

INSTRUCTIONS

1. Heat the mustard oil in a pan until it starts to smoke and changes colour. After it cools down a bit, add the sliced onions and fry them until reddish-brown.
2. While the onions are frying, wash the okra, pat it dry it and cut it in small, even pieces.
3. Add the cumin and dry red chillies to the frying onions.
4. Add the okra and turmeric. Cook, uncovered on medium heat for 10-12 minutes, or until the okra softens. Give it a good stir occasionally.
5. Add salt just when the okra is done. Serve hot with Indian naan or rice.

NOTES

1. Make sure the okra is dry before you cut it.
2. Don't add any water during the cooking process.
3. Add salt towards the end when the okra is cooked.
4. It is preferable to use a non-stick pan for this recipe.

Palak Sabzi

Ingredients

- 2 tablespoons Oil
- ½ teaspoon Cumin seeds
- 1 medium or 1 cup Red onion chopped
- 1 Green chili finely chopped
- ½ teaspoon Ginger paste or freshly grated or crushed
- ½ teaspoon Garlic paste or freshly grated
- 2 medium or 2 cups Potatoes peeled and cubed
- ¼ teaspoon Turmeric powder
- Salt to taste
- 1 teaspoon Red chili powder
- 1 teaspoon Coriander powder
- 2 cups Spinach (Palak) washed, chopped and tightly packed
- ⅓ cup Tomato chopped

Instructions

1. Heat the oil in a pan or kadai on medium heat. Once hot add cumin seeds and let them sizzle a bit and they get a little darker in color.
2. Add chopped onion and sprinkle a little salt to speed up the cooking process. Cook until onion starts to soften and becomes light pink in color.
3. Then add ginger, garlic and green chili. Saute for a minute or until the raw smell of ginger garlic goes away.
4. Add cubed potatoes, remaining salt, turmeric powder, red chili powder and coriander powder. Mix well so spices are coated evenly on the potatoes.
5. Cover the pan and cook until potatoes are 80% cooked. You may need to check and stir once or twice in between to make sure that potatoes are not sticking to the bottom of the pan.
6. Add chopped spinach and tomato. Mix, cover and cook until potatoes are 100% cooked (fork-tender). Meantime, spinach will also get cooked and tomatoes becomes soft (but not mushy).
7. Turn off the stove and keep the palak sabzi covered for 5 minutes before serving to let the flavors mingle

Bharwa Bhindi

Ingredients

- 40 pieces Okra (Bhindi) medium size
- 4 tablespoons Oil
- ⅓ cup Desiccated coconut
- 2 tablespoons Peanuts Ground into powder
- 1 tablespoons Sesame seeds
- ⅓ cup Cilantro or coriander leaves chopped
- 1 Green chili chopped finely
- ½ teaspoon Ginger paste or freshly grated or crushed
- 1 teaspoon Turmeric powder
- 1 ½ teaspoons Coriander powder
- ½ teaspoon Cumin powder
- 1 teaspoon Red chili powder
- 1 teaspoon Garam masala
- 3 teaspoons Sugar
- 2 tablespoons Lemon juice
- Salt to taste

Instructions

1. To make the stuffing, take dry coconut, ground peanuts, sesame seeds, green chili, ginger and cilantro in a bowl. Mix well.
2. Add salt, sugar, lemon juice and spice powders (turmeric powder, red chili powder, coriander powder, cumin powder, garam masala).
3. Mix everything really well using your fingers and keep it aside.
4. Now cut off both the ends (head and tail part). Make a vertical slit in the center, but be careful not to break the bhindi into two pieces.
5. Now using your one hand hold the bhindi and insert the thumb inside the slit, so it makes a gap in the bhindi to fill the stuffing. After stuffing all of them you will have leftover stuffing; we will use that later in this recipe.
6. Heat the oil in a pan on medium heat. I recommend using a wide non-stick pan because non-sticks require less oil and we can arrange them in one layer if it is wide. If not using the nonstick then you might need more oil. Alternately, you can cook them in an air fryer (see the details below in the notes section).
7. Once hot arrange stuffed okra and sprinkle some salt (be careful we already added salt to the stuffing).
8. Cover it and cook it for 12-15 minutes or until okra is cooked perfectly. Stir or flip the okra in between for even cooking. Make sure that okra doesn't stick to the bottom.
9. Add remaining leftover stuffing and mix well. Cook it for 2 minutes uncovered or until added stuffing gets heated through

Gavar Sabji

Ingredients

- 1 tablespoon Besan (gram flour)
- 1 teaspoon Red chili powder
- ¼ teaspoon Turmeric powder
- 1 teaspoon Coriander powder
- ½ teaspoon Cumin powder
- 1 ½ cups Gawar or cluster beans cut into 1 inch pieces
- 2 tablespoons Oil
- ¼ teaspoon Ajwain (Carom seeds)
- 1 Green chili chopped finely
- 2 clove Garlic chopped finely
- Salt to taste
- ½ teaspoon Amchur powder (dried mango powder)
- ½ teaspoon Garam masala

Instructions

1. Take gavar phali into a colander and rinse with water by massaging the beans lightly to remove dirt. Let the excess water drain out.
2. Remove the head and tail parts. While removing those if you find any strings then try to remove them and discard. Then cut into 1-inch pieces.
3. To prepare the steamer, add a glassful of water to a saucepan. Place a steamer pan and cover it with a lid. Let the water come to a simmer. Once it starts simmering, add chopped gavar and cover the pan with a lid.
4. Steam for 5-8 minutes or until beans are soft and tender. Remove it from the pan and keep it aside.
5. While beans are steaming, prepare the besan-spice mixture. Take besan and spice powders (turmeric powder, red chili powder, coriander powder and cumin powder) in a small bowl. Mix and keep it ready.
6. Heat the oil in a pan or kadai on medium heat. Once hot add ajwain and let them sizzle a bit. Add chopped garlic and green chili. Saute for 30-40 seconds or until the raw smell of garlic goes away.
7. Add besan-spice mixture. Immediately mix and cook by stirring constantly for 1-2 minutes.
8. Add steamed gavar and salt. Mix everything well and cook for 2 minutes.
9. Lastly, add garam masala and amchur. Mix well. Turn off the stove and gavar sabji is ready to serve

Lauki Sabzi

Ingredients

- 2 tablespoons Oil
- 1 teaspoon Mustard seeds
- 1 teaspoon Cumin seeds
- 1 Green chili finely chopped
- 10-12 Curry leaves
- ½ teaspoon Turmeric powder
- a pinch or ⅛ teaspoon Hing (Asafoetida)
- 500 grams or 4 cups Lauki (bottle gourd or dudhi) peeled and chopped
- Salt to taste
- ½ teaspoon Garam masala
- 1 tablespoon Cilantro or coriander leaves chopped finely

Instructions

- Heat the oil in a pan or kadai on medium heat. Once hot add mustard seeds and let them splutter.
- Add cumin seeds and let them sizzle a bit.
- Add green chilies and curry leaves. Saute for 30 seconds.

- Add hing and turmeric powder, and mix.
- Immediately add chopped lauki and salt. Mix well.
- Cover the pan with a lid and cook until lauki is soft and tender. Do stir once or twice in between. Lauki has a lot of moisture, so while cooking it leaves some water so there are fewer chances that sabzi will stick to the bottom of the pan.
- Once cooked, add garam masala and chopped cilantro.
- Mix well, turn off the stove and lauki ki sabji is ready to serve.

Methi Bhaji

Ingredients

- 1 ½ tablespoons Oil
- ½ teaspoon Cumin seeds
- 1 tablespoon Garlic finely chopped
- 1 large Green chili finely chopped
- ¼ teaspoon Turmeric powder
- ⅛ teaspoon Hing (Asafoetida)
- 1 cup Red onion chopped
- Salt to taste
- ¼ - ½ teaspoon Red chili powder
- 2 cups Fenugreek leaves (methi leaves)
- ⅛ teaspoon Sugar optional

Instructions

- Heat the oil in a pan or kadai on medium heat.
- Once hot add cumin seeds and let them sizzle.
- Next fry in chopped garlic and green chili till raw smell of garlic goes away or for a minute.
- Add hing and turmeric powder, immediately add onion.
- Mix and cook till onion gets soft.
- Add salt and red chili powder, mix and cook for a minute.
- Mix in methi leaves and cook for 3-4 minutes or till methi leaves gets cooked.
- If adding sugar then add at this time and stir.

Sookhi Moong Dal

Ingredients

- ½ cup Yellow moong dal (split and skinless)
- 1 tablespoon Oil
- ¼ teaspoon Mustard seeds
- ½ inch Cinnamon stick
- 2 Cloves
- 1 Dried red chilies
- ¼ teaspoon Turmeric powder
- ½ teaspoon Red chili powder
- ½ teaspoon Cumin powder
- ½ teaspoon Coriander powder
- Salt to taste
- ½ cup + 2 tablespoons Water
- 1 teaspoon Lemon juice

Instructions

- Wash and soak the dal for 30 minutes. Then discard the soaking water.
- Heat the oil in pressure cooker on medium heat. Once hot add mustard seeds. As soon as they splutter, add cloves, cinnamon and dried red chili. Saute for 30 seconds.
- Add moong dal, all the spice powders and salt, mix well.
- Add water and stir.
- Cover the cooker with lid, put the weight on and cook for 2 whistles.
- Once pressure releases, open the lid and fluff up the dal.
- Lastly squeeze the lemon juice, mix and serve.

Palak Paneer Bhurji

Ingredients

- 50 gm Spinach Leaves (Palak)
- 200 gm Paneer (Indian Cottage Cheese)
- 1 Small Onion
- 2 Medium Sized Tomatoes
- 1-2 Green Chillies

- 2-3 Cloves of Garlic
- ~1 Inch Piece of Ginger
- 1 Teaspoon Cumin Seeds (Jeera)
- 1/2 Teaspoon Turmeric Powder (Haldi)
- 1 Teaspoon Red Chilli Powder
- 1/2 Teaspoon Garam Masala
- 1 Teaspoon Salt, or to taste
- 2 Teaspoons Lemon Juice
- 2 Teaspoons Oil

Instructions

- Heat oil in a pan and add cumin seeds (jeera) in it. Roast the cumin seeds for a few seconds.
- When the cumin seeds start crackling, add some finely chopped onions, finely chopped green chillies, minced ginger & garlic.
- Fry for 3-4 minutes on medium heat till the onions turn golden brown.
- Add finely chopped tomatoes to the pan.
- Stir occasionally and cook for 4-5 minutes till the tomatoes become soft.
- Add turmeric powder (haldi), red chilli powder, garam masala and salt to the pan.
- Stir to mix and roast the spices for a couple of minutes.
- Add chopped spinach leaves to the pan.
- Mix well with the masala and let it cook. The leaves will start leaving water.
- Cook till the water is dried up and the spinach leaves are cooked.
- Add crumbled or grated paneer to the pan.
- Mix well and cook for a couple of minutes. In the end, sprinkle some lemon juice on top and mix again.
- Palak Paneer Bhurji is ready. Serve it hot with roti, naan or rice.

Note : you can play with flavours with seasonal vegetables , Add Readymade sauces in dry curry , or use different seasonings to get unique flavour nowdays there are multiple options available start implementing it we can not replace seasonal available vegetables, Grains etc but we can give international taste to any vegetarian curry

CHAPTER THIRTEEN

Salads

How to Make Salad

Start with Greens: Start with a base of greens, whether baby spinach or shredded lettuce. Try not to expect the kids to eat a ton of greens and chop them up into small pieces.

Add Cheese: If your kiddo does dairy, definitely add some cheese. Choose from shredded cheese, goat cheese crumbles, diced cheese, cheese curds or whatever kind they like most!

Add Fruit: A little sweetness goes a long way in a salad so I almost always add fruit! Think of what would taste good to you—strawberries, grapes, shredded apples, and pears are often a good fit. Or dried fruit like cranberries or golden raisins!

Watch Sizes and Textures: If your kiddo can't get chew raw snap peas or cucumbers, leave them out! Or, offer just one tiny bite of something if you aren't yet sure about how well they can chew it. (My two year old can chew a small piece of a fresh snap pea but cannot chew a whole one—she winds up spitting it out unless I cut them tiny for her.) Refresh yourself on choking hazards as needed and remember that their salad does not need to look exactly like yours!

Serve it Deconstructed: It's easier for kids to eat salad if they can easily see what's in their serving, so I recommend serving it deconstructed, or at least separated out a bit. This also makes it much easier for them to pick up components to eat them.

Add Dressing or Dip: Depending on the kid, it might work better to serve the dressing as a dip in a separate container or plate compartment, or tossed (sparingly!) with the salad. Ranch is usually a hit, though my kids have surprised me by liking tangier vinaigrettes so try a range.

VEGETABLES or FRUITS to add to a salad

BEETROOT The red vegetable increases blood circulation, drop BP and helps increase exercise endurance

Tomatoes Has Lycopene which is great on Skin and Immunity. It helps boost breathing function

Cucumbers Light, water based and soothing on the gut. More cucumber makes you eat lesser and helps beat Acidity in the gut

Onions Wash onions and your breath will smell lesser, but its so cool for the bacteria in your Gut and and makes digestion easier

Salad leaves Any type of green leaves is packed with nutrients. Lettuce, salad leaves or even SPINACH are great additions to boost quality of Fullness from a salad

Carrots Carrots have the highest content of Phosphorus which is good for cellular metabolism or giving you great energy levels. Carrots are great for SKIN and hair.

Raddish High in Vitamin C and radishes helps flush toxins out of your body via kidneys. So a perfect vegetable to clean your BODYS filters the kidneys everyday

Cabbage For those with Ulcers and injuries or inflammation, cabbage is like a natural Band-AID that helps heal you faster due to its SULHPUR content.

RAJMA Now not a vegetable but 1 cup of rajma has enough of protein post a workout session. To protein power your salad, use chick peas or rajma or any beans instead of PANEER!.

Easy salad

INGREDIENTS

- 1 cup - 250ml
- For mixing
- Pomegranate - 1/4 cup
- Sweet corn kernels - 1/3-1/2 cup
- Grated coconut – 1-2 tbsp
- Cucumber - 1 tbsp (Optional)
- Coriander leaves – 2tsp
- Pepper powder – 1/2 tsp (optional)
- Salt - as needed
- Lemon juice - few drops (optional)

HOW TO MAKE SALAD - METHOD

- Pressure cook the sweet corn and remove the kernels (Click here to see the easy removal of kernels). Finely chop the cucumber, coriander leaves. Grate the coconut using a peeler so that it looks like long strands as you see in the picture.
- In a wide bowl, add all the ingredients. Mix well, add salt and lemon juice if desired

Kakdi Koshimbir

Ingredients

- 4 small Persian cucumbers
- 1 tablespoon ghee
- 1 teaspoon cumin seeds lightly crushed in the palm of your hand
- ⅛ teaspoon asafetida ** hing (optional)
- 1 small green chili sliced lengthwise
- 1 teaspoon kosher salt
- 1 teaspoon sugar
- 2 tablespoons peanuts roasted and ground
- 2 tablespoons cilantro chopped finely for garnish

Instructions

- Peel the cucumbers, finely dice and keep in a medium bowl.
- Heat ghee in a small saucepan over medium heat. Lightly crush cumin seeds in the palm of your hands and add to the hot ghee. Allow the cumin seeds to sizzle, about 30 seconds. Add hing and green chili and cook for another 30 seconds.
- Pour the tempering on the chopped cucumbers. Add salt, sugar, peanuts, and cilantro. Mix well and serve immediately.
- If making ahead of time, hold on the salt and sugar and add them just before serving. This helps the cucumber not release too much water.

Sprouted Mung Bean Salad

Ingredients

- ½ cup sprouted mung beans
- ½ cup tomatoes diced
- ½ cup red onion diced
- ½ cup sweet corn fresh or thawed frozen
- ½ cup cucumber peeled and diced
- ½ cup carrots grated
- 1 tablespoon fresh lime juice
- ½ teaspoon Kashmiri red chili powder
- 1 teaspoon kosher salt
- ½ teaspoon chat masala optional
- ¼ cup cilantro finely chopped

Instructions

- In a medium bowl add sprouted mung beans, tomatoes, red onion, corn, cucumber, and carrots. You can also add diced avocado, jalapenos, etc
- Add red chili powder, salt, and chat masala.
- Pour the lime juice and mix well. Garnish with cilantro.

Spicy Mango Salad

Ingredients

- 2 large mangoes firm-ripe
- 2 persian cucumbers
- 1 medium red onion
- ½ cup cilantro chopped
- ½ cup roasted peanuts rough chopped, optional
- 2 to 3 tablespoons alfood mango white balsamic vinegar
- 1 to 2 tablespoons green chili olive oil
- salt to taste

Instructions

- Peel and cut the mango into 2-inch X ¼-inch sticks. Peel and cut cucumbers into 2-inch X ¼-inch sticks. Thinly slice onion
- Add chopped mangoes, cucumbers and onion to a medium bow. Stir in 2 to 3 tablespoons of mango white balsamic vinegar and 1 to 2 tablespoons of green chili olive oil. Mix well. Garnish with cilantro and chopped peanuts. Serve Immediately or Chill and serve

Quinoa Salad

Ingredients

- 2 cups cooked quinoa
- 1 can black beans rinsed and drained
- 1 cup frozen sweet corn thawed
- 1 cup grape tomatoes cut into small pieces
- 2 cucumbers peeled and diced

- 1 or 2 Jalapeños diced
- 1 medium red onion diced
- 1 red Bell Pepper diced
- 1 semi ripe mango peeled and diced
- 1 avocado diced
- ½ cup cilantro chopped
- **Dressing**
- ⅓ cup extra virgin olive oil
- 2 teaspoons kosher salt
- 2 limes juiced
- black pepper or paprika to taste

Instructions

- In a large bowl add the main ingredients.
- In a small bowl, whisk together olive oil, salt, lime juice, and black pepper or paprika.
- Pour the dressing over the salad and mix everything together to evenly coat the salad with the dressing.

Pattagobhi Salad

Ingredients

- 2 cups Pattagobhi thinly sliced and chopped
- ½ cup red pepper thinly sliced
- ½ cup green pepper thinly sliced
- ½ cup carrots julienned
- ½ cup red onion thinly sliced
- ½ cup purple cabbage. thinly sliced and chopped optional
- 1½ tablespoons oil
- 1 teaspoon black mustard seeds
- ¼ teaspoon asafetida
- ½ teaspoon ground turmeric
- ½ teaspoon red chili powder
- 1 teaspoon kosher salt
- 1 lemon cut into half & juiced

Instructions

- Mix all the veggies in a medium bowl.
- Heat oil in a small saucepan over medium heat. Once the oil is hot and shimmering, add mustard seeds and allow them to pop. Turn the heat off once the mustard seeds start to pop. Add asafetida, turmeric & red chili powder.
- Pour this tempering over the veggies. Add salt and lemon juice. Mix well

CHAPTER FOURTEEN

Finger Food for Short Break

Ravioli Pops

Ingredients

- 1/2 cup dry bread crumbs
- 2 teaspoons pepper
- 1-1/2 teaspoons dried oregano
- 1-1/2 teaspoons dried parsley flakes
- 1 teaspoon salt
- 1 teaspoon crushed red pepper flakes
- 1/3 cup all-purpose flour
- 1 spoon Corn flower mixed in one cup water
- 1 package (9 ounces) refrigerated cheese ravioli
- Oil for frying
- Grated Parmesan cheese, optional
- 42 lollipop sticks
- Warm marinara sauce and prepared pesto

Directions

1. In a shallow bowl, mix bread crumbs and seasonings. Place flour and eggs in separate shallow bowls. Dip ravioli in flour to coat both sides; shake off excess. Dip in corn flower wash, then in crumb mixture, patting to help coating adhere.
2. In a large electric or cast-iron skillet, heat 1/2 in. oil to 375°. Fry ravioli, a few at a time, until golden brown, 1-2 minutes each side. Drain on paper towels. Immediately sprinkle with cheese if desired. Carefully insert a lollipop stick into the back of each ravioli. Serve warm with marinara sauce and pesto.

Mixed vegetable kebabs

Ingredients

1 tbsp olive oil

2 small zucchini, thickly sliced

1 red capsicum, 2cm dice

1 yellow capsicum, 2cm dice

1 red onion, 2cm dice

2 cups cherry tomatoes

2 tbsp reduced salt soy sauce*

1 tbsp honey

1 clove garlic, chopped

Variations

300g cottage cheese or firm tofu, drained, 2cm cubes

Method

Combine the soy sauce, honey and garlic and set aside.

Skewer just vegetables or a combination of tofu and vegetables or pork and vegetables. Brush each kebab lightly with olive oil.

Heat a pan until hot. Add the kebabs and cook, turning on each side, until the vegetables are soft.

Brush with the soy sauce mix and cook for a further minute. Remove and serve hot.

Tip:

When chopping the ingredients, make sure everything is about the same size, so they cook evenly.

WALNUT LADOO

Ingredients

- Walnuts - ½ cup
- Dates - ½ cup or 6-7 big dates
- Poha/Beaten Rice/ Aval - ½ cup
- Cardamom powder - ¼ tsp
- Ghee - 1 tbsp

Instructions

- Measure and keep all ingredients ready. Deseed and chop dates roughly. Dry roast poha in a pan until crisp for 2-3 minutes. Remove from the pan once done.
- In the same pan, add walnuts and dry roast until its hot to touch. Switch off the flame and Cool it down. Firstly, grind the poha and walnuts in a blender along with cardamom powder to a coarse powder.
- Then add chopped dates to a blender and give a run so that dates gets mixed with powdered walnuts.

- Add a tablespoon of ghee in a pan, add dates poha walnuts mix and fry it in low flame for 2-3 minutes or until the dates is soft. Switch off the flame once done and cool it down.
- When the mixture is still warm, start making balls. Store it in an airtight container once done.

Banana Ladoo

Ingredients

- 1 glass Matta Rice or Red Rice
- 3 Cardamoms
- 1/2 tsp Cumin Seeds
- 4 Bananas (overripe)
- 1 tsp Ghee/Butter
- 10 tbsp Jaggery Grated or as required
- 1/4 tsp Dry Ginger Powder (optional)
- 2 pinches of Salt

Directions

- Firstly, take a glass of matta rice and wash it twice or thrice using water
- Keep it aside and allow it to drain off the water for 30 minutes
- Now we are going to roast the drained rice. For that heat a pan and add the drained rice.
- Roast the rice over a medium-high flame with continuous stirring until the rice turns its color.
- At this stage, turn the flame to low and add 3 cardamoms, and 1/2 tsp cumin seeds.
- Roast them again for 30 seconds and switch off the flame. Transfer it to another plate and allow it to cool down completely.
- Once cooled transfer to a mixie jar and grind to a fine powder. Transfer to another bowl and keep aside.
- Now, heat 1 tsp ghee in a pan
- Chop the bananas and add them to the hot pan. Mash the bananas using the ladle and mix them.
- Once the heat starts to get in the bananas it will start to loosen. Saute for 7 to 8 minutes until the banana thickens as shown.
- Now add 1/2 cup of grated jaggery and mix well. (Amount of jaggery depends on your sweet taste.)
- Then add 2 pinches of salt and 1/4 tsp dry ginger powder. Mix them and lower the flame.
- Start adding the ground rice powder little by little. I added nearly, 1/2 of the ground rice powder.
- Mix it and switch off the flame.Transfer it to bowl. Once it is slightly cooled, start kneading and see if the dough is sticky. If so, add some more rice powder and mix them until it turns non-sticky. Non-sticky dough is ready.

- Pinch small amount of dough and roll them to small sized balls.
- Coat it with rice powder and serve them
- Delicious banana balls are ready

VEG ARANCINI

INGREDIENTS
For Making Rice Balls

- 2 cup Dal Khichdi (leftover)
- 1 small Onion finely chopped
- 2 Garlic pods finely minced
- 1 Green Chilli
- 1 tbsp Coriander leaves
- 1 tsp Paparika powder or any chilli powder
- 2 - 3 tbsp bread crumbs
- 3/4 cup mozzarella cheese grated
- 1/4 tsp Garam Masala
- 1 pinch Salt (optional as cheese and khichdi both has salt)
- 1/2 tsp Italian mixed herb (Oregano)
- For coating & frying
- 5 - 6 tbsp bread crumbs
- 1/2 tsp Oregano
- 1/2 tsp Paparika powder
- 2 tbsp refined flour
- 1 tbsp corn starch
- 3 - 4 tbsp Water
- 1 cup Oil for deep frying

INSTRUCTIONS

- Mash the leftover khichdi completely
- Add all ingredients mentioned under making balls to the mashed khichdi
- Knead to mix all ingredients properly. Make it like a soft dough
- Greese your palms and take out small portions of lemon and roll it to smooth ball
- Make all balls and keep aside in the refrigerator to set

- Cover the box with a cling wrap or a cover when storing in refrigerator.
- You can prepare the mixture well ahead and refrigerate overnight.
- Prepare a mixture of breadcrumbs, paparika and oregano for final coating of arancini balls
- Prepare a slurry of refined flour, corn starch mixed together with water. It should be of flowing consistency
- Take a ball and drop it in the mixture of flour and amke sure its wet with the thin paste or sluury
- Take out and roll on the bread crumbs mixture. Repeat this for all balls and keep aside
- Heat oil in a pan and deep fry them till they are golden brown in color. Take out from oil and keep on paper napkin
- Serve these yummy crispy and cheesy bites with any of your favorite dip or sauce

CRISPY CORN CHAAT

INGREDIENTS

- 200 gms Sweet corn kernels Boiled
- 2 tbsp refined flour
- 2 tbsp Corn flour
- 2 tbsp garlic finely chopped
- 1 Onion finely chopped
- 1 cup Oil
- 1 tbsp Vinegar
- 1/2 tsp Salt
- 1 tsp Red Chilli Powder
- 1 tsp Lemon Juice (optional)
- 1 pinch Turmeric powder

INSTRUCTIONS

- Boil corn kernels and cool it before adding any flour to it.
- Once its cold enough, add refined flour and corn flour to it. Mix well. If required add 1 tbsp water but don't add more water. Just make sure the flour should only coat the corns.
- Heat oil in a deep frying pan. Drop the kernels into hot oil. But careful as it might burst spilling the oil all over.
- Cover the pan to avoid such condition.
- Once the corns are done they will float on the surface of oil. remove them from oil and place on paper napkin
- Heat another pan and add 2 tbsp oil. Add chopped onion and garlic and saute till translucent.
- Add red chilli powder, turmeric powder and fried corns. Add pinch of salt, vinegar and saute for 2 minutes.
- Remove from heat and add chopped coriander leaves and serve hot

POTATO LOLLIPOP

INGREDIENTS

- 4 medium potatoes Boiled, cooled, mashed
- 1/2 cup bread crumbs (brown or white)/ panko crumbs
- 1 tsp onion powder or finely chopped fresh onion
- 1 tsp garlic powder or ginger garlic paste
- 1 tbsp cilantro finely chopped
- 1/2 tsp cayenne pepper or red chilli powder
- 1 tsp lemon juice
- 1 tsp salt or as per taste
- 1 tsp red chilli flakes
- 1 tsp oregano or Italian mixed seasoning
- 2 tbsp Refined flour for slurry
- 2 tbsp Corn Starch for slurry
- 1/2 cup Panko bread crumbs for coating
- 1 cup Refined vegetable oil or canola oil for deep frying/ shallow frying

INSTRUCTIONS

1. Take mashed potatoes in a mixing bowl.
2. Add bread crumbs, onion powder, garlic powder, chilli powder, oregano (Italian seasonings), red chili flakes, chopped cilantro, & salt.
3. Mix them well.
4. Keep in refrigerator to set for sometime. This helps in binding properly.
5. Then greese your palms and take out small balls from the mixture.
6. And roll it to a ball shape or any other shape of your choice.
7. Make slurry by mixing refined flour, corn starch with 4 - 5 tbsp water. It should be of flowing consistency just for coating purpose.
8. In the meanwhile take breadcrumbs in a plate. Add chilli flakes and oregano seasoning to it. Mix well.
9. Dip the potato balls into the slurry and roll it on the panko breadcrumbs mixture.
10. Repeat this for each ball and keep aside.
11. Deep fry or shallow fry them till it turns golden and crisp.
12. Serve hot with any dip of your choice

Dahi Kebab

Ingredients:

- 3 cups Yogurt (Curd/Dahi)
- 2-3 Tbsp Chickpea Flour (Besan)
- 1-2 Green Chillies
- 2 Tbsp chopped Nuts (almonds, cashews, pistachios) (Optional)
- 1 Tbsp Coriander leaves
- Salt to taste
- Oil to fry

Method:

1. To make hung curd, place a muslin cloth on a strainer and add the yogurt. Tie the cloth and either leave in the strainer for 4-6 hours or tie the cloth over the sink. You can also leave this in the fridge overnight.
2. 3 cups of yogurt will yield 1 cup of hung curd. Take the hung curd in a large bowl.
3. Add all the ingredients except the oil and mix well.
4. Heat oil in a frying pan for shallow frying.
5. Wet your hands and take a small ball of batter and shape it as a kebab.
6. Gently place the kebab in the frying pan. If you are unable to shape the kebabs, you can use two spoons and spoon the kebabs into the frying pan.
7. Cook on medium heat.
8. Flip when the first side browns.
9. Cook until the second side is cooked too.
10. Serve hot with mint coriander chutney or ketchup.

Fried Pitod

Pitod belongs to the state of Rajasthan. Thin gram flour batter is cooked and then set and cut into the desired shape and used in the desired manner; when fried with mustard seeds, green chilies, and curry leaves, it becomes fried pitod.

Ingredients

- 2 cups pitod
- 1 tsp oil
- 1 tsp mustard seeds
- 2 slit green chilies
- A handful of curry leaves

- Lots of chopped fresh coriander leaves
- Juice of 1 lemon

Instructions for :Fried Pitod Recipe

1. This recipe serves 4 persons.
2. Heat 1 tsp mustard seeds (raie). Let it splutter.
3. Next goes in a handful of curry leaves. Cook for 30 seconds.
4. Chili time, add in 2 slit green chilies. Cook for 30 seconds.
5. Finally add in 2 cups pitod.
6. Cover and cook for 3-4 minutes.
7. Switch off the flame. Add a handful of chopped coriander leaves and lemon juice. Toss well.

Idli Dhokla

Ingredients
For Khaman/Dhokla:

- 5 cup gram flour (besan)
- 2 tbsp semolina (sooji)
- Juice of 1 lemon
- 2 tbsp powdered sugar
- 1-1.5 cups lukewarm water
- 1 tsp oil
- Salt to taste
- ¼ tsp turmeric powder
- 1 tsp ginger paste
- 1 tsp green chili paste
- 1 tsp fruit salt (Eno) + 1 tsp water

For Tempering:

- 2 tsp oil
- 1 tsp mustard seeds (raie)
- A handful of curry leaves (kadi patta)
- Pinch of asafetida (heeng)

- 2 green chilies
- ¾ cup water
- 1 tbsp powdered sugar
- Juice of half lemon

For garnishing:

- A handful of chopped coriander leaves

Instructions

1. This recipe makes 12-14 idlis.
2. Place a large sieve on a mixing bowl. Add 1.5 cups gram flour (besan) and 2 tbsp semolina (sooji). Sieve it.
3. Add lukewarm water gradually. Make a smooth batter. It calls for more than 1 cup and less than 1.5 cups of lukewarm water.
4. Mix well.
5. Next, add in 2 tbsp of powdered sugar and juice of 1 lemon.
6. Let the batter rest for 15-20 minutes. Meanwhile, grease the idli mold and pour in water in the idli maker and let it come to boil.
7. After the batter has rested, add 1 tsp oil and salt to taste and ¼ tsp turmeric powder. I forgot to add the turmeric powder, therefore added later.
8. Further, add 1 tsp each ginger paste and green chili paste.
9. Next goes in 1 tsp of fruit salt (Eno) and 1 tsp of water. Whisk it well in one direction for 30 seconds. The batter should double in size and should be absolutely spongy.
10. Fill in the idli molds.
11. Steam for 7-9 minutes or till done. De-mould once it cools down slightly.
12. Prepare the tempering, for that heat 2 tsp of oil. Add a pinch of asafetida (heeng) and 1 tsp mustard seeds (raie). Once the mustard seeds crackle, add a handful of curry leaves and 2 green chilies. Also, add in ¾ cup of water.
13. Add the juice of 1 lemon.
14. Next goes in 1 tbsp of powdered sugar.
15. Mix well.
16. Pour over the idli khaman.

Monaco Sandwich

Ingredients:

- 12 Monaco Biscuits
- 6 tsp cheese spread
- 6 tbsp grated cheese

Instructions

1. This recipe makes 6 Monaco sandwiches.
2. Spread little cheese spread on all the Monaco biscuits.
3. Add grated cheese.
4. Cover with another biscuit.
5. Pack in cling wrap if packing for tiffin or serve immediately.

Paneer Cutlet

Ingredients
For mixture

- ¾ cup crumbled paneer
- 2 small boiled potatoes, mashed
- ½ cup bread crumbs + as much required
- 1 and ½ tsp chaat masala powder
- 1 tsp white pepper powder
- Salt to taste
- A handful of chopped coriander leaves

For slurry

- 2 tbsp corn flour
- 1 tbsp all-purpose flour (maida)
- ¼ tsp white pepper powder
- Salt to taste
- ¼ cup water

For frying cutlets

- Oil, as much required

Instructions

1. This recipe makes 6-8 paneer cutlets.
2. In a mixing bowl add ¾ cup crumbled paneer, 2 boiled and mashed potatoes, a handful of chopped coriander leaves, 1 and ½ tsp chaat masala, 1 tsp white pepper powder and salt to taste.
3. Next add ½ cup bread crumbs.
4. Mix everything well. Divide into portions. Shape into cutlets.
5. Prepare the slurry by mixing together 2 tbsp corn flour, 1 tbsp all-purpose flour, ¼ tsp white pepper powder, salt to taste.
6. Add ¼ cup water and make absolutely smooth slurry.
7. Dip the cutlet in the slurry.
8. Thereafter put in a bowl or plate of bread crumbs and coat with crumbs.
9. Heat enough oil for shallow frying. Put in hot oil.
10. Fry till golden brown.

Thalipeeth

Ingredients

- 3-4 garlic cloves, peeled
- 1 green chili, chopped
- 1 tsp coriander seeds
- ½ tsp carom seeds
- ¾ tsp salt or salt to taste
- ½ cup jowar flour
- 2 tbsp wheat flour
- 2 tbsp gram flour
- 2 tbsp soaked flattened rice (poha)
- ½ onion, chopped
- A handful of chopped coriander leaves
- ¼ tsp turmeric powder
- Oil for frying
- Ghee for greasing

Instructions

1. This recipe makes 2 standard-sized thalipeeth or 3 smaller ones as I made.
2. In a mortar pestle or small grinder jar add in 3-4 garlic cloves, 1 chopped green chili, 1 tsp coriander seeds, ½ tsp carom seeds (ajwain), and salt to taste.
3. Grind to a coarse mix.
4. In a mixing bowl add in 1 cup of jowar atta, a ¼ cup of wheat atta, ¼ cup chickpea flour, ¼ cup soaked poha, ½ medium-sized onion chopped, a handful of chopped coriander leaves, ¼ tsp turmeric powder and the coarse mix prepared in step 3.
5. Mix everything very well.
6. Make a soft dough using water. And let it rest for 10 minutes.
7. Spread a wet muslin fabric on the rolling board. Place a portion of thalipeeth dough on it. Wet your fingers with water.
8. Spread the dough.
9. Make a slightly thick thalipeeth and make a hole in the center. Meanwhile, heat an iron skillet. I made thalipeeth on the non-stick pan too. But I got a better texture with the iron tawa.
10. Lift the thalipeeth along with muslin fabric.
11. Put it on hot tawa.
12. Remove the muslin fabric.
13. Add little oil through the whole in thalipeeth.
14. Cover and let it cook for 2-3 minutes.
15. Flip and add little oil again. Cover and cook for 2-3 minutes.
16. Cook till brown patches appear on both the sides.
17. Take in n plate and grease with little ghee.
18. Serve it hot or at room temperature with pickle of your choice or yogurt.

Pachole

Healthy snack recipe from the state of Himachal Pradesh made with corn, with the flavours of ginger, garlic, and green chilli; a hint of garam masala is pachole. It is a healthy breakfast recipe as pachole are prepared by steaming. This recipe from Himachal Pradesh is ready in no time, just whip up and steam. Pachole can be fried in any ways.

Ingredients

- 3 cups f boiled sweet corn kernels
- 2 tsp freshly ground ginger garlic and chili paste
- ½ tsp garam masala powder
- ½ cup gram flour (besan)
- 2 tbsp cornflour

- ½ tsp turmeric powder
- Salt to taste
- Oil for frying

Instructions

1. This recipe serves 4-5 persons.
2. Take 3 cups of boiled sweet corn kernels in a grinder jar.
3. Make a coarse paste and transfer to a mixing bowl.
4. Add in ½ cup gram flour (besan), 2 tbsp corn flour, 2 tsp paste of ginger, garlic and green chili, salt to taste, ½ tsp garam masala powder, ½ tsp turmeric powder and salt to taste.
5. Mix well and spread on a greasing plate for steaming.
6. Steam for 15-20 minutes or till cooked.
7. Cut into squares and pan fry.
8. Pan fry till golden brown.
9. Serve hot or at room temperature.

Indian Spiced Popcorn Cauliflower

Ingredients

- 1 large head of cauliflower or 2 small heads, chopped into florets (about 6 cups)
- 3 tablespoons virgin coconut oil, melted
- 2 teaspoons garam masala
- 1 teaspoon cumin
- 1 teaspoon ground ginger
- 1 teaspoon turmeric
- 1/4 - 1/2 teaspoon sea salt
- pinch of pepper

Topping:

- 1-2 tablespoons fresh parsley or cilantro, chopped

Preparation

1. Preheat the oven to 350°F and line two baking sheets with parchment paper.
2. Place the cauliflower on the baking sheets. The smaller you chop the florets, the faster this dish will roast. Don't over-crowd the cauliflower or it won't crisp up.
3. Pour the oil over the cauliflower, and then sprinkle the spices over top. Mix with your hands or a spoon to make sure the cauliflower is well coated.
4. Roast in the over for 30-35 minutes, or until slightly crisp and golden. Top with fresh parsley or cilantro.
5. Store in an airtight container in the fridge for up to a week.

Indian and Japanese Rice Dumpling Fusion

Ingredients

- 1/4 cup jaggery, grated
- 1/4 cup grated fresh coconut
- 1 cup glutinous rice flour/dango powder
- 1/2 cup, plus 1 tablespoon water
- A pinch of salt
- 1/3 cup kinako/roasted soy flour
- 2 tablespoons sugar
- Water, to boil the dango and cool it

Preparation

To Make the Coconut Filling:

1. In a small pan, combine the jaggery and coconut. Keep stirring until the jaggery dissolves and all the liquid evaporates. Remove from heat and let cool completely.

To Make the Dango Dough:

1. Mix together the glutinous rice flour, a pinch of salt, and water until it comes together into a dough.

To Fill the Dango:

1. Take a small piece of the dough, make a ball, flatten it, and place a small amount of filling in it. Seal the edges and roll into a ball again. Repeat with the remaining dough and filling.

2. In the meantime, put a large pot of water to boil. Take another bowl of cool water and set it aside to blanch the cooked dango in.

To Make the Dango:

1. Drop the filled dango balls into the boiling water, cover, and cook until the dango balls rise to the surface.
2. Drain with a slotted spoon and blanch into the bowl of cool water.

To Assemble:

1. In a medium bowl, mix together the kinako powder and sugar. Drain the cool dango balls and drop into the kinako mix and toss to coat completely.
2. Serve immediately. Reheats pretty well in the microwave

Spicy Mashed Potato Donuts

Ingredients

- ½ cup mashed potatoes
- ½ cup grated tofu
- 1 cup bread crumbs fresh
- 2 cloves garlic minced
- 2 tbsp onion finely chopped
- 2 tbsp grated carrot
- ½ tbsp paprika powder
- ½ tbsp pepper powder (freshly crushed)
- salt to taste

Instructions

1. In bowl, take all ingredients (mashed potato, tofu, bread crumbs, garlic minced, onion, carrot, paprika powder, pepper powder, salt). Mix them well. And try to maintain consistency of mixture for making ring shape
2. Put the mixture on refrigerator for 10 minutes.
3. Now make shape of ring doughnuts from mixture. You can make around 6-8 doughnuts from this quantity.
4. Now in small bowl, take 1 tbsp corn flour and dilute it into water and make corn flour slurry form it.
5. In another plate take bread crumbs for coating.

6. Take one doughnut, dip it into corn flour slurry, do the coating of bread crumbs. And fry them to medium hit.

Chickpea Patties

Ingredients

1 260g can drained chickpeas
200 g or 1 cup chopped sweet potato/butternut/potato
1 large white onion, chopped
3 cloves garlic
1 Tbsp ground flax seeds mixed with 3 Tbsp hot water
2 tsp stock powder (or more depending on salt preference)
Ground course black pepper
1 tsp English/Dijon mustard
2 Tbsp fresh chopped mixed herbs
1 Tbsp lemon juice
½ tsp bicarbonate of soda
4 heaped Tbsp potato starch/corn flour/wheat gluten
Some olive oil

Cooking Instructions

- Sweat the chopped onion, garlic and vegetables in a pan with some olive oil. Flavour to taste and cook til soft and dry.
- Blend the chickpeas until coarse and place in a mixing bowl.
- Add the vegetables, fresh herbs, lemon juice and stock powder and flax egg. Mix well.
- Add the starches/gluten with the bicarbonate of soda and mix well. Let the mixture rest for an hour or so.
- Use a spoon and dish out onto a frying pan coated with cooking spray. Shape in a round circle and bake for a minute or so til golden brown. Turn over.
- You can place them on a baking tray and bake in the oven til cooked.

Sweet Corn Patties with Mozzarella Cheese

Ingredients

- 1 cup sweet corn kernels boiled and roughly blended (150 gm)
- ⅓ cup capsicum finely chopped
- ⅓ cup green onion finely chopped
- 1 green chili finely chopped

- ½ tbsp ginger paste
- salt to taste
- 1 tbsp chat masala or garam masala
- 50 gm mozzarella cheese diced into small square
- 1 tbsp rice flour
- ⅓ cup water

Instructions

1. Blend the corn in a mixer to make a paste not coarse paste, just roughly blend it without using any water.
2. Transfer mixture into bowl and all remaining ingredients capsicum, green onion, green chilli, ginger paste, salt and chat masala.
3. Divide Mixture into 10-12 equal portions and using hand make flat base, put 1 cheese cube into it, cover cheese by whole mixture and seal it.
4. Same way, prepare all other balls or flat ball form remaining portions.
5. In small bowl, take rice flour and add ⅓ cup water and dilute rice flour into water and create batter. Consistency of batter is thick enough to cover ball outer layers so that balls. will not disintegrate while you are frying them.
6. Heat the oil in a deep non-stick to fry ball, Deep corn kebab into batter and put it into frying pan. Fry it on medium heat till its color turns into golden brown.
7. Sweet Corn Cheese patties are ready to serve; you can serve with mint-coriander chutney or also with tomato ketchup.

Palak Poha Cutlet

Ingredients

- 2 cups flattened rice (poha)
- 3 medium sized potatoes, boiled, peeled, refrigerated and grated
- Salt to taste
- 1 tsp chaat masala
- 1 tsp red chilli powder
- 1 tsp grated ginger
- 1 cup tightly packed spinach (palak), washed thoroughly and chopped
- 1 green chilli, chopped
- 2-3 tbsp rice flour (chawal ka aata)
- Oil for frying

Instructions

1. Take 1 cup flattened rice (poha) in a large bowl. Wash them. Add approx ½ cup water.
2. Leave aside for 5-6 minutes, so that the poha softens.
3. Drain away the water and let the soft poha dry out. (Tip: It is important that the poha dries out. You can even spread it on a plate or kitchen towel)
4. Transfer to a mixing bowl. Add 3 boiled and grated potatoes. (Tip: Refrigerated potatoes will give crisp cutlets), 1 tsp grated ginger, 1 tsp dry mango (amchur) powder, 1 tsp red chilli powder.
5. Mash and mix all the ingredients well.
6. Add 1 cup chopped spinach and 1 chopped green chilli.
7. Add salt to taste.
8. Add 2 tbsp rice flour (chawal ka aata).
9. Mix to form dough.
10. Check the seasoning and adjust the same if required.
11. Shape the dough into cutlets.
12. Heat 2-3 tsp oil in a pan.
13. Fry cutlets on medium flame till golden brown from both the sides.
14. Remove on an absorbent paper.
15. Serve with tomato ketchup.

Sooji Balls

Ingredients

For Sooji Balls:

- 1 cup semolina (sooji)
- 2 ½ cups water
- 2 tsp oil
- 1 tsp ginger chili paste
- ¼ cup desiccated coconut
- Salt to taste
- 1 tsp red chilli flakes
- ¼ tsp turmeric powder
- Handful of chopped coriander leaves
- Juice of 1 lemon

For tempering:

- 1 tsp oil
- 1 tsp mustard seeds
- 1 sprig curry leaves

Instructions

1. Dry roast 1 cup semolina (sooji)
2. Add salt to taste, ¼ turmeric powder, 1 tsp red chilli flakes, 1 tsp ginger chilli paste, handful of chopped coriander, ¼ cup desiccated coconut
3. Add juice of 1 lemon and 2 tsp oil
4. Mix everything well
5. Add 2 ½ cups water
6. Stirring continuously. Ensure there are no lumps. Bring the dough together
7. Cover and let it cook on low flame for 3 minutes
8. After 3 minutes, take out in a mixing bowl or plate and let it cool down till it is warm and workable
9. Knead for 5 minutes
10. Make smooth dough. Make sure it is not too soft
11. Make lemon size balls with the dough
12. Steam balls for 15 minutes
13. Take them out and let them cool

To temper sooji balls:

1. Heat 1 tsp oil
2. Add 1 tsp mustard seeds (raie)
3. Once the seeds crackle, add 1 sprig of curry leaves
4. Add steamed sooji balls
5. Sauté well for 3-4 minutes
6. Bon Appétit: Serve sooji balls with tomato ketch up and coconut chutney

Tadka Pasta

Ingredients

- 1 cup Penne or Shortcut Pasta
- 2 teaspoon vegan butter or coconut oil
- 1/2 teaspoon Mustard seeds
- 1/2 teaspoon Cumin seeds
- 1-2 Dry Red Chilies, broken
- 6-8 curry leaves

- 1 medium Onion, thinly sliced
- 2 Garlic cloves, finely minced
- 3 cups Spinach, chopped
- 1 cup Cooked Chickpeas
- 1/2 teaspoon Garam Masala, optional
- Salt to taste

Preparation

- Cook pasta accordingly to package instructions. Drain the pasta and reserve the cooking liquid.
- In a pan, melt the vegan butter/oil and add the mustard, cumin seeds, red chilies and curry leaves; once the seeds start pop, add the onions and garlic. Cook until fragrant and the onions are getting lightly browned around the edges.
- Add spinach and chickpeas; cook till spinach is wilted, about 3~4 minutes.
- Season with salt and add the pasta. Stir in the pasta cooking water to get the desired consistency.

Other Quick Options

Roasted Makhana or you can pan toss with seasonings of your choice: The search for a good substitute for junk snacks like chips and puffs never gets over. Thankfully, there is a good alternative in the form of makhana. For the health-conscious, it is a low-calorie option that is full of many nutrients like protein, potassium, carbohydrate, fiber, and minerals like magnesium, iron & zinc.

- Peri Peri Makhana
- Cream & Onion Makhana
- Pudina & Salted Makhana
- Paprika Makhana

Beaten Moong: This snack has been sold on the streets of India since always and is now finally getting its much-deserved recognition. Now available as a packaged snack, you can easily buy beaten moong from a shop near you, or online. You can consider it in your healthier quick Indian snacks list.

Dry Fruits: Our parents and grandparents have always insisted that we should eat some dry fruits on a daily basis. And, without a doubt, the health benefits of dry-fruits are many. Almonds, pistachios & cashews are some of the popular dry-fruits that are easily available

Protein Bars: When we think of protein bars, we assume that they will be a packaged bars made with many synthetic ingredients. But, you can also formulate an Indian version of protein bars with household ingredients like

Gur, almonds, honey, murmure & channa, etc. So, they are the best example of healthy Indian packaged snacks.

Fruits: Unlike many other parts of the world, India has always been known to have higher levels of fruit consumption. Having fruits at any time of the day can boost your energy levels and provide your body with all the essential nutrients that keep it healthy.

Wheat Masala Mathri: You can prepare it at home (baked option is good if you don't want fry version)

Soya Baked Chips

Baked Oats Chips

Baked Jowar Chips

Khakhra

Quinoa Coin Khakhra

Oats Coin Khakhra

Printed by Libri Plureos GmbH in Hamburg,
Germany